Managing and Maintaining a Microsoft® Windows Server™ 2003 Environment (70-290)

Lab Manual

Mark Fugatt

PUBLISHED BY
Microsoft Press
A Division of Microsoft Corporation
One Microsoft Way
Redmond, Washington 98052-6399

Printed and bound in the United States of America.

6 7 8 9   QWT   8 7

Distributed in Canada by H.B. Fenn and Company Ltd.

A CIP catalogue record for this book is available from the British Library.

Microsoft Press books are available through booksellers and distributors worldwide. For further information about international editions, contact your local Microsoft Corporation office or contact Microsoft Press International directly at fax (425)
936-7329. Visit our Web site at www.microsoft.com/learning. Send comments to *moac@microsoft.com*.

Program Managers: Linda Engelman, Hilary Long
Project Editor: Lynn Finnel
Technical Editor: Eric Dettinger

Sub Assy Part No. X10-23971
Body Part No. X10-23976

CONTENTS

LAB 1: **Understanding the Role of Microsoft Windows Server 2003** **1**

Scenario 1

Exercise 1-1: Installing Windows Server 2003 2

Exercise 1-2: Installing Active Directory and Domain Name Service (DNS). 10

Exercise 1-3: Copying the Directory Structure for the Lab 17

Exercise 1- 4: Directions for Making Screen Captures. 17

Lab Review Questions 18

LAB 2: **Administering Microsoft Windows Server 2003** . .**19**

Scenario 19

Exercise 2-1: Getting Familiar with Windows Server 2003 20

    Logging On and Logging Off Windows Server 2003 20

    Viewing System Properties 20

    Accessing the Help and Support Utility 21

    Properly Shutting Down the Computer. 21

Exercise 2-2: Creating an Organizational Unit and User Object in Active Directory 22

Exercise 2-3: Using the Microsoft Management Console (MMC) 22

Exercise 2-4: Using Remote Desktop Connection 24

Exercise 2-5: Using Terminal Services 25

Lab Review Questions 26

Lab Challenge 2-1: Administering a Server Remotely 27

LAB 3: **Monitoring Microsoft Windows Server 2003** **29**

Scenario. 29

Exercise 3-1: Using Task Manager to Monitor Windows Server 2003 30

Exercise 3-2: Using the Performance Console 31

Exercise 3-3: Using Event Viewer 33

Exercise 3-4: Creating and Viewing an Alert 34

Exercise 3-5: Using the Ping Command to Trigger Network Activity . .35

Lab Review Questions 36

Lab Challenge 3-1: Configuring the Performance Console 36

LAB 4: **Backing Up and Restoring Data** **37**

Scenario 37

Exercise 4-1: Backing Up and Restoring a Directory Using the Normal Backup Type 38

Backing Up Data 38

Restoring Backed-Up Data 39

Exercise 4-2: Backing Up and Restoring a Directory
Using the Incremental Backup Type 40

Exercise 4-3: Backing Up and Restoring a Directory Using
the Differential Backup Type. 41

Exercise 4-4: Scheduling a Backup 43

Lab Review Questions 45

Lab Challenge 4-1: Backing Up the System State Data. 45

LAB 5:   Maintaining the Operating System **47**

Exercise 5-1: Installing the Microsoft Baseline Security
Analyzer 1.1.1. 48

Exercise 5-2: Running the Microsoft Baseline Security
Analyzer 1.1.1. 48

Exercise 5-3: Preparing Your Machine to Install
Microsoft SUS. 49

Exercise 5-4: Running the Microsoft Baseline Security
Analyzer 1.1.1 to Identify New Security Risks 50

Exercise 5-5: Installing Microsoft Software Update
Services SP1 50

Exercise 5-6: Managing Licensing. 50

Switch to Per-Device or Per-User Licensing 51

Modifying the Licensing Replication Interval to 12 Hours 51

Exercise 5-7: Administering Site Licenses 51

Starting the License Logging Service 51

Adding Licenses 52

Lab Review Questions 52

Lab Challenge 5-1: Installing a Microsoft Service Pack. 53

Lab Challenge 5-2: Installing a Microsoft Hotfix 53

LAB 6:   Working with User Accounts **55**

Exercise 6-1: Creating an Organizational Unit Structure 56

Exercise 6-2: Creating Domain User Accounts 56

Exercise 6-3: Adding Information to
an Existing Account 57

Exercise 6-4: Modifying User Logon Restrictions 57

Exercise 6-5: Managing Multiple Users 58

Exercise 6-6: Importing User Accounts
from a CSV File. 59

Exercise 6-7: Moving Users 59

Exercise 6-8: Creating and Using a Template Account. 60

Exercise 6-9: Managing User Profiles 61

Lab Review Questions 62

Lab Challenge 6-1: Using Dsadd.exe and Dsmod.exe. 62

TROUBLESHOOTING LAB A: Reviewing Your Environment **65**

 Lab Dependencies 66

 Changing the Computer Configuration 66

 Troubleshooting 67

  Break Scenario 1 67

  Break Scenario 2 67

LAB 7: Working with Groups **69**

 Lab Dependencies 69

 Exercise 7-1: Raising the Functional Level
 of Your Domain 70

 Exercise 7-2: Creating Global Security Groups 70

 Exercise 7-3: Creating Domain Local Security Groups 71

 Exercise 7-4: Creating Groups Using DSADD 72

 Exercise 7-5: Adding Members to the Group 73

 Exercise 7-6: Adding Global Groups to Domain Local
 Groups 75

 Exercise 7-7: Using Dsget to Find Group Memberships 76

 Lab Review Questions 76

 Lab Challenge 7-1: Changing the Scope of a Group 76

 Lab Challenge 7-2: Using Dsmod to Add Members
 to a Group 77

LAB 8: Working with Computer Accounts **79**

 Exercise 8-1: Creating Computer Accounts Using Active Directory
 Users and Computers 80

 Exercise 8-2: Creating Computer Accounts Using Dsadd 81

 Exercise 8-3: Deleting, Disabling, and Resetting Computer
 Accounts 81

 Lab Review Questions 82

 Lab Challenge 8-1: Changing the Properties of Computer Accounts . 82

LAB 9: Sharing File System Resources **83**

 Lab Dependencies 83

 Exercise 9-1: Creating a Shared Folder 84

 Exercise 9-2: Viewing the NTFS and Share Permissions on
 a Directory 85

 Exercise 9-3: Connecting to the Share from the Run Command and
 Mapping a Drive to the Share 85

 Exercise 9-4: Setting Share Permissions 86

 Exercise 9-5: Setting NTFS Permissions 89

 Exercise 9-6: Viewing Effective Permissions 91

 Exercise 9-7: Disabling Anonymous Access
 on the Default Web Site 93

 Exercise 9-8: Taking Ownership of a File 95

Lab Review Questions 96

Lab Challenge 9-1: Adding a File to the Company
Intranet and Setting Permissions 97

LAB 10:   **Working with Printers** **99**

Lab Dependencies 99

Exercise 10-1: Creating a Locally Attached Printer 100

Exercise 10-2: Configuring the Properties
for a Local Printer 102

Exercise 10-3: Sharing a Printer 103

Exercise 10-4: Connecting to a Printer 105

Exercise 10-5: Managing a Print Queue. 107

Exercise 10-6: Monitoring a Print Queue Using
Performance Monitor. 108

Exercise 10-7: Clearing a Printer Queue 112

Lab Review Questions 112

Lab Challenge 10-1: Creating a Printer Pool. 112

LAB 11:   **Managing Device Drivers.** **113**

Exercise 11-1: Configuring Driver Signing Options 114

Exercise 11-2: Installing an Unsigned Device Driver 115

Exercise 11-3: Managing Device Properties. 117

Exercise 11-4: Using Last Known Good Configuration. 118

Lab Review Questions 119

Lab Challenge 11-1: Using Device Driver Rollback 119

LAB 12:   **Managing Disk Storage.** **121**

Lab Dependencies 121

Exercise 12-1: Creating a New Extended Partition 122

Exercise 12-2: Creating a New Logical Drive 123

Exercise 12-3: Converting a Disk from Basic to Dynamic 125

Exercise 12-4: Creating a Simple Volume 127

Exercise 12-5: Extending a Simple Volume 128

Lab Review Questions 129

Lab Challenge 12-1: Error-Checking and
Defragmenting a Volume 129

TROUBLESHOOTING LAB B: **Reviewing Your Environment.** **131**

Lab Dependencies 132

Changing the Computer Configuration. 132

Troubleshooting. 133

Break Scenario 1 133

Break Scenario 2 133

LAB 1

UNDERSTANDING THE ROLE OF MICROSOFT WINDOWS SERVER 2003

This lab contains the following exercises and activities:

- Exercise 1-1: Installing Windows Server 2003
- Exercise 1-2: Installing Active Directory and Domain Name Service (DNS)
- Exercise 1-3: Copying the Directory Structure for the Lab
- Exercise 1-4: Directions for Making Screen Captures
- Lab Review Questions

SCENARIO

You work as a network support specialist for Contoso, Ltd. Currently, the company has a small peer network. Your job is to install Windows Server 2003 and install Active Directory.

After completing this lab, you will be able to:

■ Install Windows Server 2003 from the CD

■ Install Active Directory

Estimated lesson time: 100 minutes

EXERCISE 1-1: INSTALLING WINDOWS SERVER 2003

Estimated completion time: 60 minutes

Your manager assigns you the task of installing Windows Server 2003 on a computer. You need to perform a clean installation of Windows Server 2003 on the computer.

> **MORE INFO**   This exercise is identical to the installation procedure outlined in the textbook. If you or your instructor installed Windows Server 2003 using the instructions outlined in Chapter 1, you can skip this exercise.

1. Insert the Windows Server 2003 installation CD into the CD-ROM drive, and then restart the computer. If you are prompted to do so, press a key to boot from the CD.

2. After the computer starts, a brief message appears, stating that Setup is inspecting your computer's hardware configuration. The Windows Setup screen appears.

3. If your computer requires special mass storage drivers that are not part of the Windows Server 2003 driver set, press F6 when prompted and provide the appropriate drivers.

4. The system prompts you to press F2 if you want to perform an Automated System Recovery (ASR). Do not press F2 at this time. The setup continues.

NOTE **Automated System Recovery**   ASR is a new feature in Windows Server 2003 that replaces the Emergency Repair Disk feature of previous Windows versions. For more information on using ASR, see Chapter 5 in the textbook.

The gray status bar at the bottom of the screen indicates that Setup is loading files. This is required to start a minimal version of the operating system. At this point, the hardware in the computer has not been specifically identified, so after loading the operating system kernel, the setup program loads a series of drivers that support a wide range of mass storage, keyboard, pointer, and video devices, in an attempt to create a functional input/output (I/O) configuration that will allow the installation to proceed.

NOTE **Locating Storage Drivers**   If appropriate drivers for your mass storage devices are not included with Windows Server 2003, you must obtain them, restart the installation, and then press F6 to supply them to the setup program.

5. If you are installing an evaluation version of Windows Server 2003, the Setup Notification screen appears, informing you of this. Read the Setup Notification message, and then press Enter to continue. The Welcome To Setup screen appears.

```
Windows Server 2003, Standard Edition Setup

    Welcome to Setup.

    This portion of the Setup program prepares Microsoft(R)
    Windows(R) to run on your computer.

       •  To set up Windows now, press ENTER.

       •  To repair a Windows installation using
          Recovery Console, press R.

       •  To quit Setup without installing Windows, press F3.



  ENTER=Continue   R=Repair   F3=Quit
```

6. Read the Welcome To Setup message, and then press Enter to continue. The Windows Licensing Agreement screen appears.

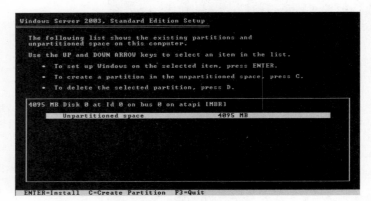

7. Read the licensing agreement, and press F8 to accept it. A screen appears, containing a list of the partitions on the computer's available disk drives as well as any unpartitioned space. From this screen, you can also create and delete partitions on the computer's drives as needed. Selecting an Unpartitioned Space entry in the list creates a new partition using all of that space. If you want to create a partition using only part of the unpartitioned space, press C and specify the size of the partition you want to create. To complete the exercises in this book, a partition of at least 3 GB is recommended. In addition, you must leave at least 1 GB of unpartitioned space on the drive for exercises that involve the creation of new partitions.

8. Select an area of unpartitioned disk space at least 4 GB in size, and then press C and specify 3072 as the size of the new partition. Press Enter.

9. A screen appears, prompting you to select the file system to use when formatting the selected partition. Select the Format The Partition Using The NTFS File System option, and press Enter to continue.

Setup formats the partition using NTFS, examines the hard disk for phys-
ical errors that might cause the installation to fail, and begins copying files
from the CD to the hard disk. This process takes several minutes.

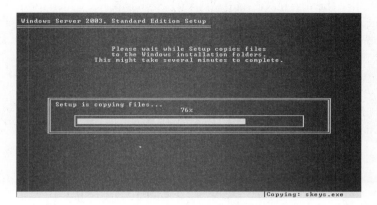

10. Setup initializes the Windows configuration and then displays a screen
    with a red status bar that counts down for 15 seconds before the com-
    puter restarts and enters the GUI mode phase of the installation process.

Windows Setup launches and produces a graphical user interface that
tracks the progress of installation in the left pane. The Collecting Information, Dynamic Update, and Preparing Installation options are selected,
indicating that these steps have been completed. Collecting Information
was completed before the GUI appeared, and Dynamic Update is not
used when you start from the CD.

The Preparing Installation step occurred when the Setup program copied the operating system files to the local disk drive. The Installing Windows step begins with Setup's hardware detection process, which might take several minutes. Unlike the text mode hardware detection routine, which identifies hardware components by loading drivers using trial and error, this process identifies the specific components in the computer, writes information about them to the registry, and configures the operating system to load the correct drivers for the hardware. Eventually, the Windows Setup wizard loads and the Regional And Language Options page appears.

11. Modify the default regional and language option settings, if necessary, by clicking the Customize button or the Details button. Then click Next. The Personalize Your Software page appears.

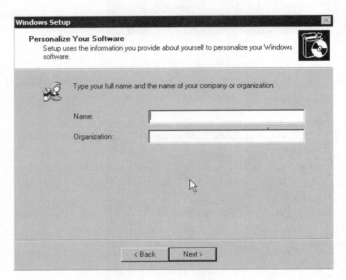

12. In the Name text box, type your name; in the Organization text box, type the name of an organization. Click Next. The Your Product Key page appears.

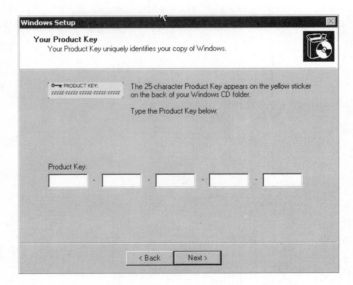

13. Enter the product key included with your Windows Server 2003 installation CD in the Product Key text boxes, and then click Next. The Licensing Modes page appears.

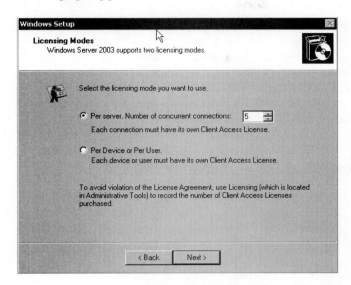

14. Leave the default value of 5 in the Per Server Number Of Concurrent Connections option, and then click Next. The Computer Name And Administrator Password page appears.

NOTE **Windows Server 2003 Licensing** If you are using an evaluation version of Windows Server 2003, the default value of 5 servers is sufficient to complete this course. However, if you are using a licensed copy of Windows Server 2003, you should specify a legal number of concurrent connections based on the actual licenses that you own.

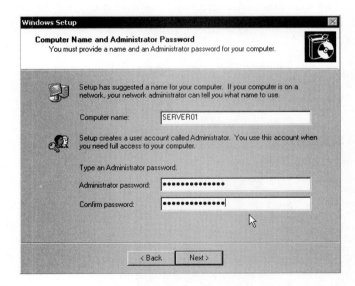

15. In the Computer Name text box, type **Server*xx***, where *xx* is a unique number assigned to you by your instructor.

CAUTION **Avoiding Name Conflicts** If your computer is connected to a LAN, check with the network administrator before assigning a name to your computer.

16. In the Administrator Password text box and the Confirm Password text box, type a password for the Administrator account, and then click Next. The Date And Time Settings page appears.

> **IMPORTANT   Specifying a Password**   In a manual installation, Windows Server 2003 prompts you to enter an administrator password that meets the complexity requirements. By default, Windows Server 2003 requires complex passwords that are at least seven characters long. A complex password is one that contains at least three of the following four elements: uppercase letters, lowercase letters, numbers, and symbols. You are allowed to enter a blank password, although this practice is strongly discouraged. A suggested password that meets the complexity requirements is MOAC@LH#1.

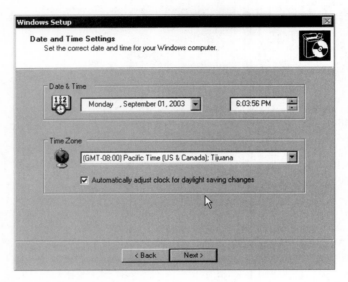

17. Specify the correct date and time, and select the correct time zone for your location. Then click Next. After a brief delay, the Networking Settings page appears.

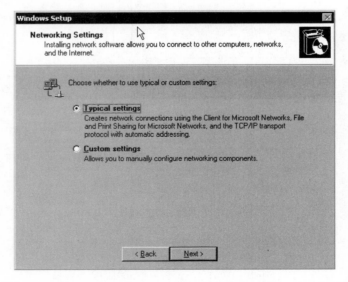

18. Leave the default Typical Settings option selected, and then click Next. The Workgroup Or Computer Domain page appears.

NOTE   Typical Networking Settings   Selecting the Typical Settings option on the Networking Settings page causes the setup program to install the Client for Microsoft Networks, Network Load Balancing, File and Printer Sharing for Microsoft Networks, and Internet Protocol (TCP/IP) components (although the Network Load Balancing module is disabled) and configure TCP/IP to obtain an IP address from a DHCP server. If you are connected to a network with no DHCP server, you must obtain an IP address and other TCP/IP configuration settings from your network administrator and select the Custom Settings option to apply them before your computer can communicate with the LAN.

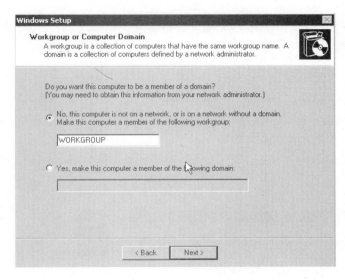

19. Leave the default No option selected and the default workgroup name of WORKGROUP in place, and then click Next.

   The setup program installs and configures the remaining operating system components by copying files, installing Start menu items, registering components, saving settings, and removing temporary files. When the installation is complete, the computer restarts automatically and the Welcome To Windows dialog box appears.

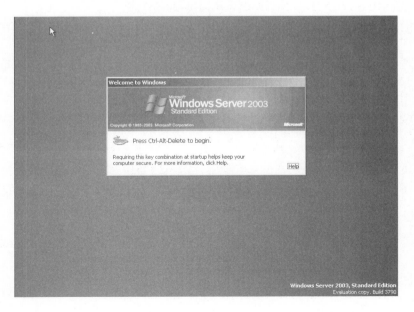

EXERCISE 1-2: INSTALLING ACTIVE DIRECTORY AND DOMAIN NAME SERVICE (DNS)

Estimated completion time: 20 minutes

Contoso has outgrown its peer-to-peer network and requires central administration of resources. You need to install the server as the domain controller, so you must install Active Directory and DNS (which is required by Active Directory) on the server.

> **MORE INFO**   This exercise is identical to the installation procedure for Active Directory outlined in the textbook. If you or your instructor installed Active Directory using the instructions outlined in Chapter 1, you can skip this exercise.

1. Log on to Windows Server 2003 as Administrator.

2. If it is not already open, open the Manage Your Server page from the Administrative Tools program group.

3. Click the Add Or Remove A Role hyperlink. The Configure Your Server wizard loads, and the Preliminary Steps page appears.

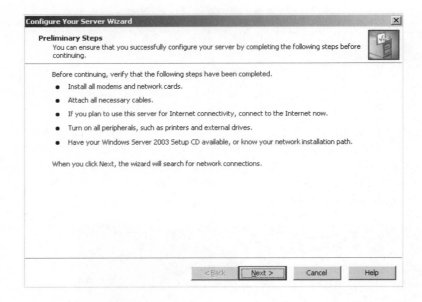

4. Verify that all of the steps listed on the page have been completed, and then click Next. After a brief delay while the wizard scans the network, the Server Role page appears.

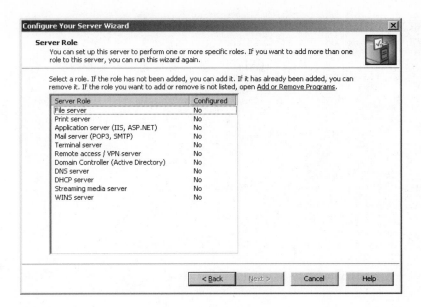

5. Select Domain Controller (Active Directory) from the list of server roles, and click Next. The Summary Of Selections page appears.

6. Click Next. The Active Directory Installation Wizard launches.

7. Click Next to bypass the Welcome page. The Operating System Compatibility page appears.

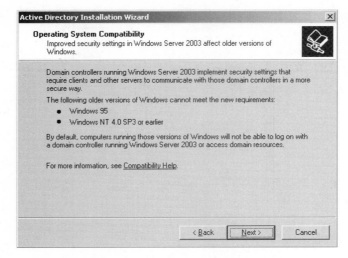

8. Read the information on the page and click Next. The Domain Controller Type page appears.

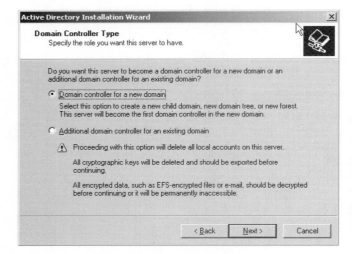

9. Leave the default Domain Controller For A New Domain option selected, and click Next. The Create New Domain page appears.

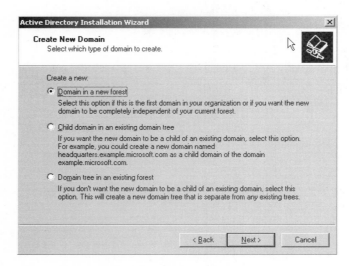

10. Leave the default Domain In A New Forest option selected, and click Next. The New Domain Name page appears.

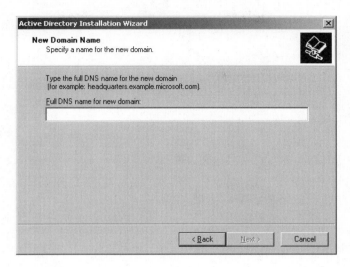

11. In the Full DNS Name For New Domain text box, type **contoso*xx*.com**, where ***xx*** is a number assigned to you by your instructor, and then click Next. The NetBIOS Domain Name page appears.

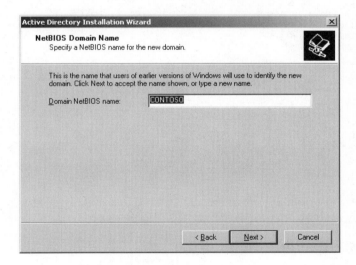

NOTE   Student Number Placeholder   Throughout this lab manual, when you are instructed to enter **Contosoxx.com, xx** is a placeholder for the student number assigned to you by your instructor.

12. Verify that the Domain NetBIOS Name text box reads CONTOSO***XX***, and then click Next. The Database And Log Folders page appears.

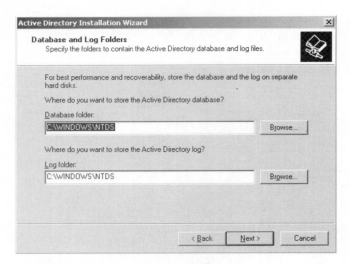

13. Click Next to accept the default database and log folder locations. The
Shared System Volume page appears.

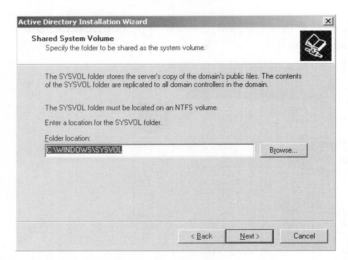

14. Click Next to accept the default shared system volume location. The DNS
Registration Diagnostics page appears.

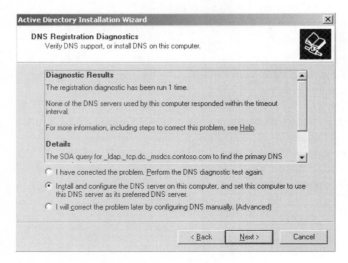

At this time, the wizard attempts to connect to the DNS servers specified in the computer's TCP/IP configuration to determine whether they are capable of hosting the records required for an Active Directory domain.

15. Select the Install And Configure The DNS Server On This Computer option, and then click Next. The Permissions page appears.

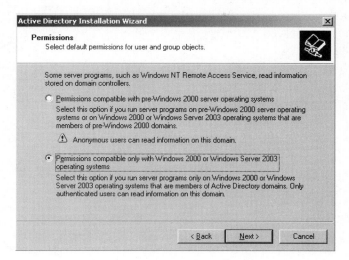

16. Click Next to accept the default permissions option, and then click Next. The Directory Services Restore Mode Administrator Password page appears.

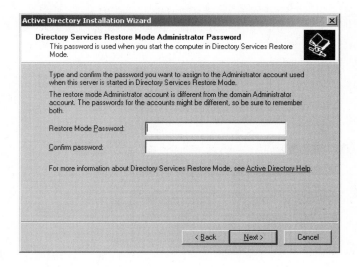

17. Type an appropriate password in the Restore Mode Password and Confirm Password text boxes, and then click Next. The Summary page appears.

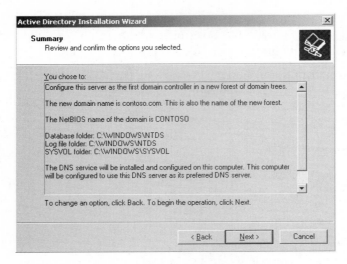

18. Review the options you have selected in the wizard, and then click Next. The wizard proceeds to install the Active Directory and DNS Server services.

    NOTE   Configuring your dynamic IP address   If your computer is configured to obtain an IP address dynamically (which is the default configuration for this course), you may receive a warning during installation of the DNS Server services. If this happens, close the Local Area Connection properties dialog box to continue using dynamically assigned IP addresses.

19. When the configuration process is finished, the Completing The Active Directory Installation Wizard page appears. Click Finish.

20. An Active Directory Installation Wizard message box appears, prompting you to restart the computer. Click Restart Now.

21. After the system has restarted, log on as Administrator. The Configure Your Server Wizard reappears, displaying the This Server Is Now A Domain Controller page.

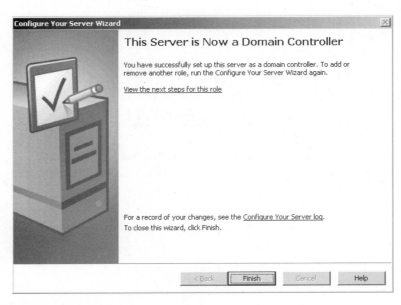

22. Click Finish.

EXERCISE 1-3: COPYING THE DIRECTORY STRUCTURE FOR THE LAB

Estimated completion time: 5 minutes

The Student CD includes a directory structure that you need to copy to your computer. This directory tree contains folders that you can use to save the files you create when you work on the lab exercises or challenges. It also contains utilities not included with the Windows Server 2003 operating system that you might be asked to install.

To copy this directory structure to your computer, follow this procedure:

1. Insert your Student CD in your CD-ROM drive.

2. Click Start, point to All Programs, point to Accessories, and select Windows Explorer. Windows Explorer opens, showing the contents of the My Documents folder by default.

3. In the directory tree in the left pane, expand the My Computer node and select the node representing your CD-ROM drive. The folder view in the right pane shows the Textbook and Lab Manual folders.

4. Select the Lab Manual folder in the folder view, and drag it to the Local Disk (C:) drive in the directory tree. The Lab Manual directory structure is copied to your drive C.

EXERCISE 1- 4: DIRECTIONS FOR MAKING SCREEN CAPTURES

Estimated completion time: 5 minutes

A screen capture is a graphic record of what is displayed on your computer screen. Making a screen capture is a good way to record information. Your instructor might also ask you to turn in certain screen captures for grading purposes. There are two basic types of screen captures: full-screen and active-window.

To make a screen capture, follow this procedure:

1. Press the Print Screen key (which is typically abbreviated as PrtScn or PrntScrn) to make a full-screen capture, or press the Alt and Print Screen keys simultaneously to make an active-window screen capture. In this course, you are usually asked to make an active-window screen capture.

2. Open MSPAINT. You can click Start, click Run, type **mspaint** in the Run dialog box, and then press Enter. Optionally, you can launch the program by clicking Start, pointing to All Programs, pointing to Accessories, and selecting Paint.

3. Press the Ctrl and V keys simultaneously to paste your screen capture. Optionally, on the Edit menu you can select Paste.

4. To save the screen capture, on the File menu select Save As to open the Save As dialog box. Notice the Save In drop-down list at the top of the dialog box. For this course, you save your screen captures in the Labwork folder for the particular lab. For example, any screen captures for this lab are to be saved in the C:\Lab Manual\Lab 01\Labwork folder.

5. Type an appropriate name for your screen capture in the File Name text box. In the Save As Type drop-down list, select the file type as specified by your instructor or leave the default .bmp file type.

6. Click Save to save your screen capture.

LAB REVIEW QUESTIONS

Estimated completion time: 10 minutes

1. A user sends you e-mail saying that he needs to install Windows Server 2003 but has a server computer that requires special mass storage drivers that are not part of the Windows 2000 Server disk set. The problem is that you must load the drivers in order for the drives to be recognized by the Installation Setup program. What should you do?

2. Why was the DNS Server service installed as part of the installation of Active Directory?

3. What is the file system type that Windows Server 2003 uses by default?

LAB 2
ADMINISTERING MICROSOFT WINDOWS SERVER 2003

This lab contains the following exercises and activities:

- Exercise 2-1: Getting Familiar with Windows Server 2003

- Exercise 2-2: Creating an Organizational Unit and User Object in Active Directory

- Exercise 2-3: Using the Microsoft Management Console (MMC)

- Exercise 2-4: Using Remote Desktop Connection

- Exercise 2-5: Using Terminal Services

- Lab Review Questions

- Lab Challenge 2-1: Administering a Server Remotely

SCENARIO

Contoso Ltd. a large multinational company with annual sales in excess of $500 million, wants to use Windows Server 2003 as its main server platform. Currently, users access the Microsoft Windows NT Server for payroll, billing, and accounting. Because Windows Server 2003 is a new platform, the manager of information technology, wants you to become familiar with elements such as creating users and running the Microsoft Management Console (MMC), so you can support users and train the other IT employees.

After completing this lab, you will be able to:

- Create an organizational unit (OU) and user object in Active Directory
- Use the runas command to run a command or utility as another user
- Use MMC
- Use Remote Desktop to control a remote computer
- Use Terminal Services Configuration and Terminal Services Manager to configure and manage remote sessions

Estimated completion time: 145 minutes

EXERCISE 2-1: GETTING FAMILIAR WITH WINDOWS SERVER 2003

Estimated completion time: 20 minutes

You are new to Windows Server 2003, and your manager at Contoso, Ltd. wants you to familiarize yourself with the product so you can support the company's users. To do this, you log on and off Windows Server 2003, view system properties, view Task Manager, access the Help And Support utility, and shut down the computer.

Logging On and Logging Off Windows Server 2003

1. To log on to the computer, press Ctrl+Alt+Delete. Enter your username and password information in the appropriate text boxes.

   If the Manage Your Server window appears, select the Don't Display This Page At Logon check box near the bottom right corner of the window and close the window. Manage Your Server is located in Administrative Tools on the Start menu if you need to access it later.

2. Press Ctrl+Alt+Delete. The Windows Security dialog box appears.

3. Click the Log Off button. The Log Off Windows message box appears, with the message "Are you sure you want to log off?"

4. Click Log Off. You are logged off, and the Welcome To Windows window appears.

Viewing System Properties

1. Log back on to the computer. Click Start, point to Control Panel, and click System. The System Properties dialog box appears.

2. Select the General tab if it is not already displayed. The General tab displays system, registration, and computer information.

3. Record the system information.

4. Record the computer information.

5. Select the Computer Name tab.

6. Record the full computer name.

7. Record the domain name.

8. Close the System Properties dialog box.

Accessing the Help and Support Utility

1. Click Start, and select Help and Support. The Help And Support Center window appears. Note that some of these tools require an Internet connection because they access the Microsoft Web site.

2. In the Help Contents section on the left, click the Welcome hyperlink. Click a few other links to familiarize yourself with the online help.

3. Click the Home button.

4. In the Support Tasks section on the right, click the Tools link.

5. Now let's perform a search. In the Search text box, type **shutdown**, and then click the adjacent arrow. The Search Results window appears.

6. Locate and click the link labeled "Restart or shut down locally and document the reason: Shutdown Event Tracker." The right pane opens with the text "To restart or shut down locally and document the reason," allowing you to choose between the Using The Windows Interface and Using A Command Line links.

7. In the right pane, click the Using The Windows Interface link.

8. Record the steps for shutting down your computer.

9. Close the Help And Support Center window.

Properly Shutting Down the Computer

1. Click Start, and select Shut Down. The Shut Down Windows dialog box appears.

2. In the What Do You Want The Computer To Do? drop-down list, select Restart.

3. In the Shutdown Event Tracker section, leave the Planned check box selected. Select the Other (Planned) entry from the Option drop-down list.

4. In the Comment text box, type **Rebooting for class**.

5. Click OK. Note that you cannot click OK unless you enter a comment. The computer restarts.

EXERCISE 2-2: CREATING AN ORGANIZATIONAL UNIT AND USER OBJECT IN ACTIVE DIRECTORY

Estimated completion time: 20 minutes

Your manager has assigned you the task of adding an organizational unit (OU) and user object to Active Directory.

1. Log on to the domain as Administrator with the appropriate password.

2. Click Start, point to Administrative Tools, and click Active Directory Users And Computers. The Active Directory Users And Computers console opens.

3. Expand your domain object. This is the object named contoso*xx*.com.

4. To add a new OU, right-click the domain object, point to New, and then click Organizational Unit. The New Object—Organizational Unit dialog box appears.

5. Type **ContosoOU**, and then click OK. The New Object—Organizational Unit window closes, and the new OU is created in the domain.

   QUESTION   What is the purpose of an OU?

6. To create a user account, right-click the ContosoOU object, point to New, and click User. The New Object—User wizard opens.

7. In the First Name text box, type **Test**; in the Last Name text box, type **Tester**; in the User Logon Name text box, type **TTester**. Click Next. The New Object—User wizard prompts you for a password.

8. Enter a password and confirm it.

9. Click Next. The New Object—User wizard displays summary information.

10. Click Finish. The New Object—User window closes, and the new user object is created.

11. Right-click the user object and select Add To A Group. The Select Group dialog box appears.

12. In the Enter The Object Names To Select box, type **Print Operators**, and then click OK. A message box informs you that "The Add to Group operation was successfully completed."

    MORE INFO   **User and Group Objects**   User objects are covered in more detail in Chapter 6 of the textbook, and groups are covered in Chapter 7.

13. Close Active Directory Users And Computers.

EXERCISE 2-3: USING THE MICROSOFT MANAGEMENT CONSOLE (MMC)

Estimated completion time: 15 minutes

   IMPORTANT   You must complete Exercise 2-2 before beginning this exercise. In this exercise, you use MMC to manage the local computer.

1. Click Start, and then click Run. The Run dialog box opens.

2. Type **mmc**, and then press Enter or click OK. An empty MMC console opens.

3. From the File menu, select Add/Remove Snap-In. The Add/Remove Snap-In dialog box opens.

4. Click Add. The Add Standalone Snap-In dialog box opens.

5. Scroll until you locate the Computer Management snap-in, select it, and click Add. The Computer Management window opens.

6. To use the snap-in to manage the local computer, verify that the option for the local computer is selected. Click Finish.

The snap-in named Computer Management (Local) appears in the Add/Remove Snap-In dialog box, but the Add Standalone Snap-In dialog box remains open so you can add additional snap-ins.

7. Click Close to close the Add Standalone Snap-In dialog box.

8. Click OK to close the Add/Remove Snap-In dialog box.

9. Expand the Computer Management (Local) object in the console's scope pane. The System Tools, Storage, and Services and Applications tools appear.

10. To view disk management on the local computer, click the Disk Management object beneath the Storage tool. The Disk Management tool opens. You can use this utility to manage the volumes and partitions of the disks that are directly attached to the computer.

11. To save the MMC file, click File and then click Save As. The Save As dialog box opens.

QUESTION *What is the extension of the filename?*

12. In the Save In drop-down list, browse to C:\Lab Manual\Lab 02\Labwork.

13. In the File Name text box, type **Exercise 2-3**, and then click Save. The Save As dialog box closes, and you are returned to the Disk Management tool.

14. Click File, and then click Options. The Options dialog box opens. Here you can change the mode, which governs how a user can use the MMC console.

15. Click the down arrow in the Console Mode drop-down list.

16. Scroll through the modes in the Console Mode drop-down list, and record the difference between Author Mode and User Mode—Limited Access, Single Window.

17. Click Cancel.

18. Close MMC.

19. Log off as Administrator.

20. Next you will log on as a user and issue the runas command to run a command as another user. Log on as the user you created in Exercise 2-2. The user account's logon name is TTester. If this is the first time you have logged on with this account, you must change the password because this default option was selected when the account was created.

21. Click Start and then click Run. The Run dialog box opens.

22. Enter **mmc** in the Run dialog box, and click Enter. An empty MMC console appears.

23. On the File menu, click Open. The Open dialog box appears.

24. In the Open dialog box, browse to C:\Lab Manual\Lab 02\Labwork\ Exercise 2-3, select the file, and click Open. The MMC console you saved earlier opens, and an error message appears, warning you that you don't have access rights.

25. Browse through the tools in the console. You will receive many error messages indicating that you don't have access rights or permissions to use a particular tool.

26. Close the MMC console.

27. Next you will run MMC as Administrator while still logged in as TTester. Open the Run dialog box, type **runas /user:administrator mmc**, and press Enter. The runas utility opens in a console window and prompts you to enter the administrator password.

28. Type the administrator password. An empty MMC console opens.

29. Click File, and then click C:\Lab Manual\Lab 02\Labwork\Exercise 2-3.msc. The Computer Management console opens.

30. Within Computer Management (Local), experiment with three of the tools for the local computer, but do not change anything.

QUESTION   List the three tools you used, and identify their purpose.

31. Close the MMC console without saving changes and log off.

EXERCISE 2-4: USING REMOTE DESKTOP CONNECTION

Estimated completion time: 20 minutes

Your manager wants you to enable Remote Desktop Connection on your computer and then test the connection to a remote computer. She wants this tested so you can support the desktop of the Contoso users remotely. In this lab exercise, you need access to a remote computer. Work with a partner. This exercise is to be done on both servers.

1. Click Start, point to Control Panel, and then click System. The System Properties dialog box opens.

2. In the Remote Desktop section of the Remote tab, select Allow Users To Connect Remotely To This Computer. This is required before your lab partner can connect to this computer. Perform this step on both computers before the next step. If a Remote Sessions message box opens, click OK to close it. Click OK to close the System Properties dialog box.

3. To test Remote Desktop Connection on a remote computer, click Start, point to All Programs, point to Accessories, point to Communications, and click Remote Desktop Connection. The Remote Desktop Connection dialog box opens.

4. In the Computer text box, type the IP address of your lab partner's computer. If you need to find out the IP address of your computer, open a command prompt from the Start menu and enter **ipconfig**.

5. Click Connect. The Remote Desktop Connection bar appears at the top of your screen, and you are prompted to log on to the remote computer.

6. In the User Name text box, enter **Administrator**.

7. Have your lab partner enter the Administrator password for his computer in the Password text box, and then click OK. Your lab partner's desktop appears on your screen.

QUESTION   Will the system allow you to use local programs while a Remote Desktop Connection window is open?

8. Create a folder on the desktop of the remote computer named Remote Desktop Connection Folder. The folder will be visible on the remote computer.

9. To close the remote session, click the X in the console bar at the top of the screen. The Disconnect Windows Session dialog box opens.

10. Click OK to disconnect.

11. Verify that the folder was created on your lab partner's desktop.

EXERCISE 2-5: USING TERMINAL SERVICES

Estimated completion time: 30 minutes

Your manager wants you to configure and manage remote sessions using Terminal Services. You must complete Exercise 2-4 before beginning this lab exercise. You will work with a lab partner again on this exercise.

1. Click Start, point to Administrative Tools, and click Terminal Services Configuration. The Terminal Services Configuration MMC console opens.

2. Expand the Terminal Services Configuration object in the scope pane, and select the Connections folder.

3. In the details pane, right-click the RDP-Tcp object, and then click Properties. The RDP-Tcp Properties dialog box opens.

4. Select the Always Use The Following Logon Information option in the Logon Settings tab.

5. In the User Name text box, type **Administrator**.

6. In the Domain text box, type the name of your domain. Be sure to enter your domain, not your lab partner's.

7. Select the Always Prompt For Password check box.

8. To configure the timeout settings for the connection, select the Override User Settings option in the Sessions tab. Select 5 minutes in the End A Disconnected Session drop-down list. Set the active session limit to 5 minutes, and set the idle session limit to 1 minute.

9. To ensure that there is only one active remote session, set the maximum number of connections on the Network Adapter tab to 1.

10. Click OK to close the RDP-Tcp Properties dialog box.

11. To manage the remote session, on your server click Start, point to Administrative Tools, and click Terminal Services Manager. The Terminal Services Manager MMC console opens. A Terminal Services Manager message box might also open. If so, click OK to close it.

12. Select the Users tab in the details pane. The details pane shows an object for each user logged on to your domain. There should currently be one object representing your Administrator account.

13. Have your lab partner connect to your server using Remote Desktop Connection, as in Exercise 2-4. An object representing your lab partner's Administrator account is added to the details pane. This shows the session statistics of your lab partner's remote RDP-Tcp type session.

14. Have your lab partner remain idle for at least a minute.

   QUESTION   After a minute or so, your partner should receive a message. What is the text of this message?

15. Have your lab partner click OK to reconnect to your server.

16. In the Terminal Services Manager console on your server, right-click the object representing your lab partner's user in the Server column, and click Send Message. The Send Message dialog box opens.

17. In the Message text box, type **Howdy Partner**, and then click OK. Your partner should receive the message on his server.

18. To forcibly log your lab partner off of your server, right-click the object representing your partner's user in the Server column, select Logoff, and click OK. Your lab partner is logged off and receives a message box saying that he has been logged off of the remote computer.

19. Close all windows and log off your server.

LAB REVIEW QUESTIONS

Estimated completion time: 20 minutes

1. When you first logged on using the TTester account that you created in Exercise 2-2, you had to change the password for the account. Why?

2. What is the purpose of a Domain User Account?

3. What is the purpose of Remote Desktop Connection?

4. What is the default mode of MMC, and what permission does it allow?

5. What is the purpose of Terminal Services Manager, and what tasks did you perform with it?

6. Where does a domain user account reside?

7. Name a group to which a user object can be added in order to allow the user to log on to the domain controller.

LAB CHALLENGE 2-1: ADMINISTERING A SERVER REMOTELY

Estimated completion time: 20 minutes

Contoso, Ltd. has hired an intern named Wendy Wheeler. You need to create a user account for her on the domain. You need to create a user account for her on the domain, and add her to the built-in Guest group.

You are away from the domain controller when your manager asks you to create an account for Wendy, but a colleague offers you the use of his server, which also runs Windows Server 2003. You make a connection to your domain controller, but the task takes more than 5 minutes and you receive a message saying, "The remote session ended because the total logon time limit was reached."

Create the remote connection from your lab partner's machine to yours. Configure Terminal Services so you aren't disconnected after 5 minutes, and create an appropriate account for Wendy.

MONITORING MICROSOFT WINDOWS SERVER 2003

This lab contains the following exercises and activities:

■ Exercise 3-1: Using Task Manager to Monitor Windows Server 2003

■ Exercise 3-2: Using the Performance Console

■ Exercise 3-3: Using Event Viewer

■ Exercise 3-4: Creating and Viewing an Alert

■ Exercise 3-5: Using the Ping Command to Trigger Network Activity

■ Lab Review Questions

■ Lab Challenge 3-1: Configuring the Performance Console

SCENARIO

Contoso Ltd. is in the process of converting its old billing application to a new one that will run on Windows Server 2003. Your manager is concerned about how Windows Server 2003 will react with the new billing application, which will come online in a few months. She has given you the task of monitoring Windows Server 2003 on a test basis so you can be ready for actual monitoring of the server when the billing application goes live.

Estimated completion time: 100 minutes

EXERCISE 3-1: USING TASK MANAGER TO MONITOR WINDOWS SERVER 2003

Estimated completion time: 20 minutes

Your manager has assigned you to work with Task Manager so you can help Contoso users who have task-related issues.

1. Log on to the domain as Administrator with the appropriate password.

2. Press Ctrl+Alt+Delete. The Windows Security dialog box appears.

3. Click Task Manager. The Windows Task Manager window appears.

4. Select the Applications tab. The list of applications and their status appears. Note that there might be no applications running at the moment.

5. Leave Task Manager open.

6. To start an application, click Start and then click Run. The Run dialog box opens.

7. In the Open text box, type **calc**, and then click OK. The Calculator application opens. Also, Task Manager's Applications tab shows a new task.

8. Record the task and its status.

9. In the Calculator program, click View and then click Scientific. The calculator displays additional functions.

10. Now you will cause some processor activity. In the Calculator text box, type **100** and then quickly click the X^3 key 10 to 15 times to cause the application to stop responding. After a few seconds, Task Manager shows that the Calculator's status changes.

11. Record the new status.

12. In Task Manager, right-click the Calculator task that is not responding and then click End Task. The End Program—Calculator dialog box opens.

13. Click End Now to end the task. After a few seconds, the Calculator application closes.

14. Click Don't Send to dismiss the Windows Calculator Application File dialog box without sending an error report to Microsoft.

15. Record the list of applications in the Application tab of Task Manager.

16. Click the Processes tab to display the Process page in Task Manager. Several columns will appear on the page, including Image Name, User Name, CPU, and Mem Usage.

17. You can click the column headings to sort the columns in ascending or descending order.

18. Sort the CPU column in descending order. Record the first three processes.

19. Click the Mem Usage column in descending order. Record the first three processes.

20. Select the Performance tab to look at the Performance page in Task Manager. The Performance page displays the CPU Usage History and Page File Usage History in graphs.

21. To trigger some activity, double-click the Internet Explorer icon on the taskbar at least 10 times. You might get a security message about Internet Explorer. If so, click OK. This causes the CPU graph to spike, possibly up to 100 percent. Also, you will have several Internet Explorer windows open that will need to be closed.

22. Make a screen capture of Task Manager's Performance tab and save it in C:\Lab Manual\Lab 03\Labwork as Exercise3-1.bmp.

23. Close the Internet Explorer windows and the security window if it is open.

24. Select the Networking tab to look at the Networking page in Task Manager. A graph appears with the status of your Local Area Connection. The graph goes up and down as network activity occurs on the network card.

   Record the state of your connection.

25. Select the Users tab to view the users who are logged on to the system.

26. Record the user(s).

27. To log off as Administrator, right-click the Administrator user and click Logoff. The Windows Task Manager dialog box appears, asking you to confirm that you want to log the user off.

28. Click Yes to log the user off.

29. Record what occurred.

EXERCISE 3-2: USING THE PERFORMANCE CONSOLE

Estimated completion time: 20 minutes

Your manager has assigned you the task of running the Performance console so you can learn how to troubleshoot the server for Contoso users.

1. Log on to the domain as Administrator with the appropriate password.

2. To start the Performance console, click Start, point to Administrative Tools, and click Performance.

   The Performance console opens. In the scope pane, you will see a Console Root folder containing System Monitor and Performance Logs and Alerts elements. In the details pane, a graph appears.

3. The graph contains the performance counters for three objects by default. At the bottom of the details pane, you will see three rows containing information about the counters and objects.

4. Record the objects and their associated counters. You might have to widen the columns (by clicking the vertical bar separating the column names) to view the complete names.

5. Move the Performance console around the desktop by clicking in the title bar and dragging the console around with the mouse. This causes an increase in processor usage.

6. Make a screen capture of the Performance console showing the graph for the Processor object and the % Processor counter, and save it in C:\Lab Manual\Lab 03\Labwork as Exercise3.2a.bmp.

7. To modify the properties of the % Processor counter, select the row containing this object, right-click it, and click Properties. By default, this counter is the third object in the list in the details pane.

The System Monitor Properties dialog box opens with the Data tab selected by default.

8. In the Counters section, select \Memory\Pages/sec and click Remove.

9. In the Counters section, select \PhysicalDisk(_Total)\Avg. Disk Queue Length and click Remove.

10. In the Width drop-down list, select the third width selection from the top.

11. Select the Graph tab. The Graph properties appear.

12. In the Title text box, type **My Graph**.

13. In the Vertical Axis text box, type **Percent Use**.

14. In the Show area, select both the Vertical Grid and the Horizontal Grid check boxes.

15. Click OK. The graph reflects the change.

16. To save these settings, click File and then click Save As. The Save As window opens.

17. In the Save In drop-down list, select C:\Lab Manual\Lab 03\Labwork.

18. In the File Name text box, type **MyPerformanceMonitor**, and click Save.

19. To add a counter, right-click the graph area and click Properties. The System Monitor Properties dialog box opens with the Data tab selected by default.

20. Click Add. The Add Counters window opens.

21. In the Performance Object drop-down list, select LogicalDisk. The Logical-Disk counters appear.

22. Verify that the %Disk Time counter is selected.

23. Click Explain. The Explain Text windows opens.

24. In your own words, record the explanation.

25. Close the Explain Text window.

26. Verify that the _Total instance is selected. This instance includes all of the logical drives, such as C and D.

27. Record the drive letters under the _Total instance that are included in the Total.

28. Click Add to add the LogicalDisk performance object.

29. Click Close.

The Add Counters dialog box closes. The System Monitor Properties dialog box becomes active with the new counter %Disk Time for the LogicalDisk object.

30. Click OK to close System Monitor Properties.

31. To change the color of the %Disk Time counter, right-click on the graph and click Properties.

32. Select the %Disk Time counter.

33. Click Color, and change the color to yellow.

34. Click OK to return to the graph.

35. To trigger some activity, open Windows Explorer and open and close folders and files on your local drives.

36. After a few minutes, return to the Performance window.

37. Make a screen capture of the Performance console showing the graph for the %Disk Time, and save it in C:\Lab Manual\Lab 03\Labwork as Exercise3.2b.bmp.

38. Click File, and then click Save.

39. Close the Performance console.

EXERCISE 3-3: USING EVENT VIEWER

Estimated completion time: 15 minutes

Your manager has assigned you to use Event Viewer to manage event logs.

1. To start Event Viewer, click Start, point to Administrative Tools, and click Event Viewer.

   Event Viewer opens in an MMC console. The scope pane lists the types of logs. The details pane contains details about each log.

2. Record the logs in the scope pane.

3. To view events in the System log, select the System icon in the scope pane. The list of events in the System log appears.

4. Record the event types you see in the details pane for the System log.

5. Double-click the first event in the details pane. The Event Properties dialog box opens.

6. To scroll through the events in the details pane, click the down arrow. The information for the next event entry in the log is displayed.

7. To copy the event to a file, click the button with a clipboard icon just below the down arrow.

8. To save the information in this event, click Start and then click Run.

9. In the Run window, type **clipbrd** and click OK. If you receive a message about starting the ClipBook service, click OK. The ClipBook Viewer opens with the details of the event.

10. To save this to a file, click File and then click Save As. In the Save As dialog box, select C:\Lab Manual\Lab 03\Labwork in the Save In drop-down list. In the File Name text box, type **EventViewer1**. Click Save.

11. Close the ClipBook Viewer.

12. Click OK to close the Event Properties dialog box.

13. To view the properties of the System log, right-click System in the scope pane and then click Properties. The System Properties dialog box opens, with two tabs—the General tab and the Filter tab.

14. Verify that the General tab is active.

15. Record the maximum log size in KB.

16. In the When Maximum Log Size Is Reached area, record the default value for the When Maximum Log Size Is Reached setting.

17. Select the Filter tab.

18. Record the event types that are filtered.

19. To view only Information events, uncheck all of the other events except the Information event, and then click OK.

    Only Information events are displayed.

20. To view all events, right-click the System icon in the scope pane, and click Properties to display the System Properties dialog box. In the Filter tab, select all event types and click OK. All events are displayed again.

21. Click OK to close the System Properties dialog box.

22. To clear all of the events in the System log, right-click System in the scope pane, and click Clear All Events.

    An Event Viewer message box appears, asking if you want to save the System log before clearing it.

23. Click Yes. The Save System As dialog box opens.

24. In the Save In drop-down list, select C:\Lab Manual\Lab 03\Labwork.

25. In the File Name text box, type **MySystemLog**.

26. Record the extension of the log file.

27. Click Save to save the log file. The file is saved, and the events are cleared from the details pane.

28. To view the MySystemLog file, click Action on the Event Viewer menu bar and click Open Log File. The Open dialog box opens.

29. Select the file named MySystemLog.evt, select System in the Log Type drop-down list, and click Open. The saved System log file opens as Saved System Log.

30. Close Event Viewer.

EXERCISE 3-4: CREATING AND VIEWING AN ALERT

Estimated completion time: 15 minutes

Your manager has assigned you the task of creating an alert in the Performance console and then viewing that event in Event Viewer.

1. Open the Performance console.

2. In the scope pane, expand Performance Logs and Alerts.

3. Right-click Alerts, and click New Alert Setting. The New Alert Settings dialog box appears.

4. In the Name text box, type **MyAlert**. Click OK. The MyAlert dialog box opens.

5. In the Comment text box, type **Working With Alerts**.

6. To add a performance counter, click Add. The Add Counters dialog box opens.

7. The default is the Processor object with the % Processor Time counter selected. Verify this, and click Add. The counter is added.

8. Click Close. The counter is added to the Counters area of the MyAlert dialog box.

9. Verify that the Alert When The Value Is setting is Over.

10. To trigger an alert when the Processor's time usage percentage exceeds 1 percent, type **1** in the Limit text box.

11. In the Sample Data Every Interval list box, select 1.

12. Click OK to add the alert.

13. Leave the Performance console open.

14. Open the Application log in Event Viewer.

15. Double-click the first event to open the Event Properties dialog box. You will see an event each time the %Processor Time counter exceeds 1 percent.

16. Record the actual processor percentage (the counter value).

17. Click OK to close the Event Properties dialog box.

18. In the Performance console, right-click the MyAlert alert and click Stop.

19. Record what happened to the color of the associated icon.

20. In Event Viewer, clear all events in the Application log. Right-click Application, and click Clear All Events.

21. Click No to avoid saving the Application events.

22. Close Event Viewer.

23. Close the Performance console.

EXERCISE 3-5: USING THE PING COMMAND TO TRIGGER NETWORK ACTIVITY

Estimated completion time: 10 minutes

In this exercise, you use the ping command to simulate network activity. Then you use Task Manager to view this activity. Finally, you end the process tree in Task Manager.

1. Open a command prompt. In the command prompt window, type **ping –t –l 65500 *IP_Address_of_Remote_PC***. For example, if the remote computer's IP address is 10.1.1.2, you would enter **ping –t –l 65500 10.1.1.2**. Note the use of the –t option as in "time" and the –l option as in "length." The –t option pings until you terminate it. By default, it pings only four times. The –l 65500 option sends a 65,500–byte data packet (the maximum size) instead of the default 32 bytes. Be sure to put a space between the –l and the number 65500. These two options trigger enough activity to be noticeable in the Network window of Task Manager.

2. Press Ctrl+Alt+Delete. The Windows Security dialog box appears.

3. Click Task Manager. The Windows Task Manager window appears.

4. Click the Networking tab.

5. Wait for about 1 minute so network activity can be recorded on the graph.

6. Make a screen capture of Task Manager, and save it in C:\Lab Manual \Lab 03\Labwork as Exercise3-5.bmp.

7. In Task Manager, select the Processes tab.

8. In the Image Name column, locate the cmd.exe process.

9. Right-click cmd.exe, and click End Process Tree.

10. Click Yes in the Task Manager Warning message.

11. The command prompt (cmd) and the ping command are both terminated. Because you executed the ping command from the command prompt (cmd), the ping command is considered a "child" process of the command prompt. By terminating the process tree, you terminate both cmd and ping.

12. Select the Networking tab.

13. Record the change to the graph.

14. Log off as Administrator.

LAB REVIEW QUESTIONS

Estimated completion time: 10 minutes

1. What is the purpose of Task Manager?

2. If your server is a domain controller, which logs appear in Event Viewer?

3. What can you do with the Performance console?

4. Which log file in Event Viewer are performance alerts sent to?

5. What is the purpose of filtering events in Event Viewer?

LAB CHALLENGE 3-1: CONFIGURING THE PERFORMANCE CONSOLE

Estimated completion time: 10 minutes

Configure the Performance console to monitor the Memory object with the average number of pages faulted per second, and the Processor object with the percentage of time the processor is idle. Open any file on the hard drive to generate some activity in the system. Make a screen capture showing the Performance console monitoring this activity, and save it in C:\Lab Manual\Lab 03\Labwork as Challenge3-1.bmp.

LAB 4
BACKING UP AND RESTORING DATA

This lab contains the following exercises and activities:

■ Exercise 4-1: Backing Up and Restoring a Directory Using the Normal Backup Type

■ Exercise 4-2: Backing Up and Restoring a Directory Using the Incremental Backup Type

■ Exercise 4-3: Backing Up and Restoring a Directory Using the Differential Backup Type

■ Exercise 4-4: Scheduling a Backup

■ Lab Review Questions

■ Lab Challenge 4-1: Backing Up the System State Data

SCENARIO

The users of Contoso, Ltd. handle large amounts of data during the business day, and the data on the company's Microsoft Windows 2003 servers must be protected. Your manager has assigned you the task of backing up the user data. However, she first wants you to learn various backup methods.

After completing this lab, you will be able to:

- Back up and restore a directory using the normal backup type
- Back up and restore a directory using the incremental backup type
- Back up and restore a directory using the differential backup type
- Schedule a backup

Estimated completion time: 125 minutes

EXERCISE 4-1: BACKING UP AND RESTORING A DIRECTORY USING THE NORMAL BACKUP TYPE

Estimated completion time: 20 minutes

You must test and implement the Normal backup and restoration method.

Backing Up Data

1. Log on to the domain as Administrator with the appropriate password.

2. Open Windows Explorer from the Start menu, and browse to the C:\Lab Manual\Lab 04\Labwork\BackupNormal folder. This folder contains two text files, NormalA.txt and NormalB.txt, that you will back up using the Backup utility included with Windows Server 2003.

3. To view the attributes of the files located within this folder, select Details from the View menu.

   QUESTION   What attribute is listed in the Attributes column for each file?

4. To start the backup process, click Start, point to All Programs, point to Accessories, point to System Tools, and click Backup.

   The Backup Utility opens. If this is the first time you've run the utility, it opens in wizard mode. (To prevent the utility from starting in wizard mode, clear the Always Start In Wizard Mode check box. The next time you run the utility, this initial wizard page will not appear. However, you can still access the wizard when the Backup Utility window opens.)

5. Click the Advanced Mode link to switch the utility to advanced mode. Four tabs are available in this mode, with the Welcome tab active by default.

6. Select the Backup tab. The Backup tab provides a tree view of the drives, files, and folders on your computer. Here you can select the files and folders that you want to back up, in the same way that you use Windows Explorer to select and open drives and folders.

7. In the folder tree (the left pane of the tree view), expand drive C and browse to the C:\Lab Manual\Lab 04\Labwork\BackupNormal folder.

8. Select the check box to the left of the BackupNormal folder in the folder tree. A blue check appears in the check box.

9. Click the BackupNormal folder name in the folder tree. The two file names, NormalA.txt and NormalB.txt, are displayed in the file view (the right pane of the tree view). These files also have a check mark to the left of their names.

   QUESTION   What is the significance of the check mark?

10. In the Backup Media Or File Name text box near the bottom of the Backup tab, type **C:\Lab Manual\Lab 04\Labwork\Normal.bkf**, or click Browse to browse to this location.

11. Click Start Backup. The Backup Job Information dialog box opens.

   QUESTION   What is the default setting of the If The Media Already Contains Backups option?

12. Click Advanced. The Advanced Backup Options dialog box opens.

13. Verify that Normal is selected in the Backup Type drop-down list, and click OK to close the Advanced Backup Options dialog box.

14. Click Start Backup to initiate the backup process. The Backup Progress dialog box opens. Within a minute or two, the status bar indicates the backup is complete.

15. To view the backup report, click Report. The backup log file opens in Notepad, displaying information about the backup operation.

16. Close the Notepad window.

17. Click Close to close the Backup Progress dialog box.

18. Close the Backup utility.

19. Delete the folder named BackupNormal and the files within it. In Windows Explorer, browse to the C:\Lab Manual\Lab 04\Labwork\BackupNormal folder. Right-click the folder, and select Delete.

   A message box opens, asking you to confirm the folder deletion.

20. Click Yes to confirm that you want to remove the folder and move all its contents to the Recycle Bin. The BackupNormal folder and its contents are deleted.

Restoring Backed-Up Data

Now let's restore the directory and files.

1. Open the Backup utility again, and select the Restore And Manage Media tab. The Backup utility opens to the Restore And Manage Media tab.

2. In the folder tree, click the plus sign (+) next to the File node to expand it. The backup file created earlier, Normal.bkf, appears.

3. In the folder tree, expand the Normal.bkf node until the BackupNormal folder appears. Click the folder. The files you backed up, NormalA.txt and NormalB.txt, appear in the file view.

4. Select the check box for each file in the file view.

5. Verify that Original Location is selected in the Restore Files To drop-down list.

6. Click Start Restore. The Confirm Restore dialog box opens.

7. Click OK to start restoring your data. The Restore Progress window opens. Within a minute or two, a message appears indicating that the restore is complete.

8. Click Close to close the Restore Progress window.

> **QUESTION**   Were the files restored?

9. Close the Backup utility and Windows Explorer.

EXERCISE 4-2: BACKING UP AND RESTORING A DIRECTORY USING THE INCREMENTAL BACKUP TYPE

Estimated completion time: 20 minutes

To become familiar with incremental backups, you will perform an incremental backup and note the attribute status of the files included in the backup before and after the backup process. You will then modify a file and perform another incremental backup.

1. Open Windows Explorer from the Start menu, and browse to the C:\Lab Manual\Lab 04\Labwork\BackupIncremental folder. This folder contains two text files, IncrementalA.txt and IncrementalB.txt.

2. To view the attributes of the files in this folder, select Details from the View menu.

> **QUESTION**   What attribute is listed in the Attributes column for each file?

3. Start the Backup utility in advanced mode, as described in Exercise 4-1.

4. Select the Backup tab. The Backup tab provides a tree view of the drives, files, and folders on your computer. Here you can select the files and folders that you want to back up.

5. In the folder tree, expand drive C and browse to the C:\Lab Manual \Lab 04\Labwork\BackupIncremental folder.

6. Select the check box to the left of the Backup Incremental folder in the folder tree. A blue check appears in the check box.

7. Click on the Backup Incremental folder name in the folder tree. The two filenames, IncrementalA.txt and IncrementalB.txt, are displayed in the file view. These files also have a check to the left of their name.

8. In the Backup Media Or File Name text box near the bottom of the Backup tab, type **C:\Lab Manual\Lab 04\Labwork\Incremental.bkf**, or click Browse to browse to this location.

9. Click Start Backup. The Backup Job Information dialog box opens.

10. Click Advanced. The Advanced Backup Options dialog box opens.

11. Select Incremental in the Backup Type drop-down list, and click OK to close the Advanced Backup Options dialog box.

12. Click Start Backup to initiate the incremental backup process. The Backup Progress dialog box opens. Within a minute or two, the status indicates that the backup is complete.

13. Click Close to close the Backup Progress dialog box.

14. In Windows Explorer, browse to the C:\Lab Manual\Lab 04\Labwork \Backup Incremental folder.

> **QUESTION**   *Record whether the A (for Archive) attribute is set for the files in the folder.*

15. Next you will add data to one of the files. To open IncrementalA.txt, right-click the file in Windows Explorer, and click Open. The IncrementalA.txt file opens in Notepad.

16. Type something in the file to modify its contents.

17. To save the file, select Save from the File menu.

18. Close the file by selecting Exit from the File menu.

> **QUESTION**   *Was the A attribute reset?*

19. You will now perform another incremental backup of the same folder. In the Backup utility's folder tree, browse to the C:\Lab Manual\Lab 04\Labwork \BackupIncremental folder and select the check box next to the folder's name.

20. Click Start Backup. The Backup Job Information dialog box opens.

21. Click Advanced. The Advanced Backup Options dialog box opens.

22. Select Incremental in the Backup Type drop-down list, and click OK to close the Advanced Backup Options dialog box.

23. Click Start Backup to initiate the incremental backup process. The Backup Progress dialog box opens. Within a minute or two, the status indicates that the backup is complete.

> **QUESTION**   *The Backup Progress dialog box indicates that only one file was processed. Why was only one file backed up?*

24. Click Close to close the Backup Progress dialog box.

25. Close the Backup Utility and Windows Explorer.

EXERCISE 4-3: BACKING UP AND RESTORING A DIRECTORY USING THE DIFFERENTIAL BACKUP TYPE

Estimated completion time: 20 minutes

To understand differential backups, you will perform one. You will note the attribute status before and after the backup, and then you will perform another differential backup.

1. Open Windows Explorer from the Start menu, and browse to the C:\Lab Manual\Lab 04\Labwork\BackupDifferential folder. This folder contains two text files, DifferentialA.txt and DifferentialB.txt.

2. To view the attributes of the files located within this folder, select Details from the View menu.

   QUESTION *What attribute is listed in the Attributes column for each file?*

3. Start the Backup utility in advanced mode, and select the Backup tab. The Backup tab provides a tree view of the drives, files, and folders that are on your computer. Here you can select the files and folders that you want to back up.

4. In the folder tree, expand drive C and browse to the C:\Lab Manual \Lab 04\Labwork\BackupDifferential folder.

5. Select the check box to the left of the BackupDifferential folder in the folder tree. A blue check appears in the check box.

6. Click the BackupDifferential folder name in the folder tree. Two filenames, DifferentialA.txt and DifferentialB.txt, are displayed in the file view. These files also have a check to the left of their name.

7. In the Backup Media Or File Name text box near the bottom of the Backup tab, type **C:\Lab Manual\Lab 04\Labwork\Differential.bkf**, or click Browse to browse to this location.

8. Click Start Backup. The Backup Job Information dialog box opens.

9. Click Advanced. The Advanced Backup Options dialog box opens.

10. Select Differential in the Backup Type drop-down list, and click OK to close the Advanced Backup Options dialog box.

11. Click Start Backup to initiate the differential backup process. The Backup Progress dialog box opens. Within a minute or two, the status indicates the backup is complete.

12. Click Close to close the Backup Progress dialog box.

13. In Windows Explorer, browse to the C:\Lab Manual\Lab 04\Labwork \BackupDifferential folder.

    QUESTION *Record whether the A (for Archive) attribute is set for the files in the folder.*

14. You will now perform another differential backup of the same folder. In the Backup utility's folder tree, browse to the C:\Lab Manual\Lab 04 \Labwork\BackupDifferential folder and select the check box next to the folder's name.

15. Click Start Backup. The Backup Job Information dialog box opens.

16. Click Advanced. The Advanced Backup Options dialog box opens.

17. Select Differential in the Backup Type drop-down list, and click OK to close the Advanced Backup Options dialog box.

18. Click Start Backup to initiate the differential backup process. The Backup Progress dialog box opens. Within a minute or two, the status indicates that the backup is complete.

    QUESTION *The Backup Progress dialog box indicates that two files were processed. Why were both files backed up when neither one was modified after the previous differential backup?*

19. Click Close to close the Backup Progress dialog box.

20. Close the Backup Utility and Windows Explorer.

EXERCISE 4-4: SCHEDULING A BACKUP

Estimated completion time: 25 minutes

You have been assigned the task of scheduling a backup for Contoso users. You will schedule a backup, wait for the backup to complete, delete the backed-up files to simulate data loss, and then restore the backup.

1. Open Windows Explorer from the Start menu, and browse to the C:\Lab Manual\Lab 04\Labwork\BackupNormal folder used in Exercise 4-1. This folder contains two text files, NormalA.txt and NormalB.txt.

2. To view the attributes of the files in this folder, select Details from the View menu. The A (or Archive) attribute is listed for each file.

3. Start the Backup utility in advanced mode.

4. Select the Schedule Jobs tab, where you can schedule backup jobs.

5. Click Add Job (at the bottom right of the tab). The Backup Wizard opens.

6. Click Next. The What To Back Up page of the Backup Wizard appears.

    QUESTION *What can you back up?*

7. Select the Back Up Selected Files, Drives Or Network Data option.

8. Click Next. The Items To Back Up page of the Backup Wizard appears, with a tree view of the drives, files, and folders on your computer. Here you can select the files and folders that you want to schedule for backup.

9. In the folder tree, expand drive C and browse to the C:\Lab Manual \Lab 04\Labwork\BackupNormal folder.

10. Select the check box to the left of the BackupNormal folder in the folder tree. A blue check appears in the check box.

11. Click the BackupNormal folder name in the folder tree. Two filenames, NormalA.txt and NormalB.txt, are displayed in the file view. These files also have a check to the left of their name.

12. Click Next. The Backup Type, Destination, And Name page of the Backup Wizard appears.

13. In the Choose A Place To Save Your Backup drop-down list, verify that
    C:\Lab Manual\Lab 04\Labwork is selected.

14. In the Type A Name For This Backup text box, type **Scheduled**, and then
    click Next. The Type Of Backup page of the Backup Wizard appears.

15. In the Select The Type Of Backup box, select Normal and read the
    description.

16. In the Select The Type Of Backup box, select Copy and read the description.

    QUESTION   Record the difference between Normal and Copy.

17. Because you will perform a normal backup type, select Normal.

18. Click Next. The How To Back Up page of the Backup Wizard appears.

19. Select the Verify Data After Backup check box.

20. Select the Disable Volume Shadow Copy check box.

    QUESTION   Explain what volume shadow copy is.

21. Click Next. The Backup Options page of the Backup Wizard appears.

22. Verify that the Append This Backup To The Existing Backups option is
    selected.

23. Click Next. The When To Back Up page of the Backup Wizard appears.

24. In the When Do You Want To Run The Backup options area, verify that
    the Later option is selected.

25. In the Schedule Entry area, in the Job Name text box, type **Scheduled
    Backup Job**.

26. Click Set Schedule. The Schedule Job dialog box appears.

27. Verify that Once is selected in the Schedule Task drop-down list, and set
    the Start Time to 10 minutes from the current system time. You can find
    this time on the taskbar.

28. Click OK to close the Schedule Job dialog box. The Set Account Information
    dialog box opens.

29. In the Run As text box, verify that the domain name and the administrator
    user are entered. For example, for Contoso01 and the user Administrator,
    you would enter **CONTOSO01\Administrator**.

30. Type the password for Administrator and confirm it.

31. Click OK to close the Set Account Information dialog box.

32. Click Next in the Backup Wizard. You might need to repeat steps 29
    through 31. The Completing The Backup Wizard page appears, indicating
    that the wizard has completed successfully.

33. Click Finish to close the Backup Wizard.

34. Close the Backup utility.

35. Wait for the backup job to start and complete.

36. In Windows Explorer, browse to the C:\Lab Manual\Lab 04\Labwork
    \BackupNormal folder.

QUESTION *What do you notice about the Archive attribute for the files NormalA.txt and NormalB.txt?*

37. In Windows Explorer, simulate data loss by deleting the BackupNormal folder as described in steps 19 and 20 of Exercise 4-1.

38. Now you will restore the files. In Windows Explorer, double-click the Scheduled.bkf file. The Backup utility opens.

39. Perform the restoration process using the procedure described in the "Restoring Backed-Up Data" section of Exercise 4-1, except this time you will restore the Scheduled.bkf backup file instead of the Normal.bkf backup file.

40. Log off as Administrator.

LAB REVIEW QUESTIONS

Estimated completion time: 20 minutes

1. What is the benefit of backing up data stored on disk?

2. How does the incremental backup type work?

3. Your backup schedule includes a normal backup of a hard drive every Sunday at 9 P.M. and a differential backup at 9 P.M. on all other days. You store your backups on a tape drive. If your hard drive fails on a Saturday morning, how many restore operations will you need to restore all the lost data? Explain your answer.

4. What is the purpose of volume shadow copy?

5. How can you perform a differential backup every Friday at 4 P.M. when users are still writing to data files?

6. What is the purpose of verifying your data after performing a backup?

7. Your backup schedule includes a normal backup of a hard drive every Sunday at 9 P.M. and an incremental backup at 9 P.M. on all other days. You store your backups on a tape drive. If your hard drive fails on a Saturday morning, how many restore operations will you need to restore all the lost data? Explain your answer.

LAB CHALLENGE 4-1: BACKING UP THE SYSTEM STATE DATA

Estimated completion time: 20 minutes

Your manager at Contoso wants to protect the data on the Contoso servers, particularly the system boot files and Windows registry on the Windows 2003 Server. She asks you to schedule the proper backup procedure for these files on Fridays at 9 P.M.

After you complete this challenge, make one screen capture showing the Finish page of the Backup Wizard and one screen capture showing the Schedule Jobs tab of the Backup utility. Save these screen captures in the C:\Lab Manual\Lab 04 \Labwork folder as Finish.bmp and Schedule.bmp, respectively.

LAB 5

MAINTAINING THE OPERATING SYSTEM

This lab contains the following exercises and activities:

- Exercise 5-1: Installing the Microsoft Baseline Security Analyzer 1.1.1

- Exercise 5-2: Running the Microsoft Baseline Security Analyzer 1.1.1

- Exercise 5-3: Preparing Your Machine to Install Microsoft SUS

- Exercise 5-4: Running the Microsoft Baseline Security Analyzer 1.1.1 to Identify New Security Risks

- Exercise 5-5: Installing Microsoft Software Update Services SP1

- Exercise 5-6: Managing Licensing

- Exercise 5-7: Administering Site Licenses

- Lab Review Questions

- Lab Challenge 5-1: Installing a Microsoft Service Pack

- Lab Challenge 5-2: Installing a Microsoft Hotfix

After completing this lab, you will be able to:

■ Manage a software update infrastructure

■ Manage software site licensing

Estimated completion time: 155 minutes

EXERCISE 5-1: INSTALLING THE MICROSOFT BASELINE SECURITY ANALYZER 1.1.1

Estimated completion time: 10 minutes

Your manager has asked you to install the Microsoft Baseline Security Analyzer (MBSA) on your server.

1. Log on to the computer as Administrator.

2. Open Windows Explorer, and navigate to C:\Lab Manual\Lab 05 \Tools\MBSA 1.1.1\Mbsasetup.msi.

3. Double-click Mbsasetup.msi to start the installation of MBSA. The Microsoft Baseline Security Analyzer Setup wizard launches.

4. Click Next.

5. Select the I Accept The License Agreement option, and click Next.

6. Accept the defaults on the User Information page, and click Next.

7. Accept the defaults on the Destination Folder page, and click Next.

8. Clear the Launch Application After Installation check box, and click Next.

9. Accept the defaults on the Select Features page.

10. Click Next in the Ready To Install The Application page. MBSA is installed, and a readme file opens in Microsoft Internet Explorer.

11. Once the installation has completed, click Finish to close the wizard.

12. Briefly scan through the readme file, and then close it.

EXERCISE 5-2: RUNNING THE MICROSOFT BASELINE SECURITY ANALYZER 1.1.1

Estimated completion time: 15 minutes

As part of the weekly security audit of the company's servers, you have been instructed to run MBSA on your server.

1. Click Start, point to All Programs, and select Microsoft Baseline Security Analyzer. MBSA launches.

2. Click Scan A Computer.

3. Make sure your computer is selected in the Computer Name drop-down list, and click Start Scan. MBSA starts scanning your machine for security risks.

4. Review the Security Report generated by MBSA.

5. Click the Copy link. Open Notepad, and then paste the copied information into Notepad. Save the file as C:\Lab Manual\Lab 05\Labwork\Mbsaoutput1.txt.

EXERCISE 5-3: PREPARING YOUR MACHINE TO INSTALL MICROSOFT SUS

Estimated completion time: 15 minutes

As your network has grown, it has become harder to manage and distribute updates to workstations and servers. Your manager has asked you to install Microsoft Internet Information Services (IIS) on your Microsoft Windows Server 2003 system so you can install Microsoft Software Update Services (SUS) later.

1. Run Add Or Remove Programs from Control Panel.

2. Click Add/Remove Windows Components.

3. Select Application Server. The Windows Components wizard opens.

> **CAUTION** **Selecting Individual Server Components** Do not select the check box next to Application Server because this installs all the Application Server components and you are required to install only IIS.

4. Click Details. The Application Server dialog box opens.

5. Select Internet Information Services (IIS), and then click Details.

6. Scroll to the bottom of the list, and select the check box next to World Wide Web Services.

> **QUESTION** What other options are selected in the Internet Information Services dialog box if you select World Wide Web Services?

7. Click OK to close the Internet Information Services dialog box. Click OK again to close the Application Server dialog box.

8. Click Next to start the installation of IIS. The Configuring Components page indicates the installation's progress.

> **CAUTION** **Ask Your Instructor** If a dialog box appears asking for the installation files, ask your instructor for the location of these files.

9. Click Finish in the Windows Component wizard to complete the installation of IIS.

10. Close Add Or Remove Programs.

EXERCISE 5-4: RUNNING THE MICROSOFT BASELINE SECURITY ANALYZER 1.1.1 TO IDENTIFY NEW SECURITY RISKS

Estimated completion time: 5 minutes

Your manager has asked you to run MBSA again to see if installing IIS has opened any security risks on the server.

1. Follow the steps in Exercise 5-2.

2. Review the Internet Information Services (IIS) scan results.

3. Click the Copy link, and then paste this information into Notepad. Save the file as C:\Lab Manual\Lab 05\Labwork\Mbsaoutput2.txt.

EXERCISE 5-5: INSTALLING MICROSOFT SOFTWARE UPDATE SERVICES SP1

Estimated completion time: 20 minutes

Your manager has asked you to implement Microsoft SUS on the Windows Server 2003 system.

1. Open Windows Explorer, and browse to the C:\Lab Manual\Lab 05\Tools \SUS Server 1.0 with SP1\ folder. Double-click Sus10sp1.exe to start the installation of SUS. The Microsoft Software Update Services Setup Wizard launches.

2. Click Next.

3. Select the I Accept The Terms In The License Agreement option, and click Next.

4. Click Typical in the Choose Setup Type page.

5. Click Install in the Ready To Install page. The installation of SUS begins.

6. The Completing The Microsoft Software Update Services Setup Wizard page appears. Note the URL listed in this page. (This is the URL you use to administer SUS.)

7. Click Finish. The Microsoft Software Update Services administration page opens in Internet Explorer.

8. Close the administration page.

EXERCISE 5-6: MANAGING LICENSING

Estimated completion time: 10 minutes

WARNING This lab should not be performed in a production environment. Performing this lab on a production system could cause irrevocable changes to be made to your system's licensing settings.

When your server was installed, it was configured to use per-server licensing. This worked well for a time, but the company has installed more servers and has decided to switch to per-device or per-user licensing. You must implement this change and also set replication of the licensing data for every 12 hours, to comply with company policy.

Switch to Per-Device or Per-User Licensing

1. In Control Panel, click Licensing. The Choose Licensing Mode dialog box opens.

2. Select the Per Device Or Per User option. A Licensing Violation message box opens, asking if you want to cancel the request.

3. Click No to proceed with the change to per-device or per-user licensing.

4. Click OK. The Per Device Or Per User Licensing dialog box opens.

5. Select the I Agree That check box to indicate that you have purchased Client Access Licenses (CALs) for every device or user that will access the server.

6. Click OK to complete the switch to per-device or per-user licensing.

Modifying the Licensing Replication Interval to 12 Hours

1. Click Licensing in Control Panel. The Choose Licensing Mode dialog box opens.

2. Click Replication. The Replication Configuration dialog box opens.

3. In the Start Every field, change the default of 24 hours to 12 hours. Click OK.

4. Click OK to close the Licensing dialog box.

EXERCISE 5-7: ADMINISTERING SITE LICENSES

Estimated completion time: 15 minutes

You have been assigned the task of managing the company's licensing, which recently changed from a per-server model to a per-device or per-user model. The company is hiring 25 new full-time employees and has purchased licenses for each of them, and you have been asked to add the licenses to your server.

Starting the License Logging Service

1. On the Administrative Tools menu, select Services. The Services console opens.

2. Scroll down the list of services and select License Logging.

   QUESTION   What is the current status of the License Logging service?

3. Right-click License Logging, and select Properties. The License Logging Properties dialog box opens, with the General tab active.

4. In the Startup Type drop-down list, select Automatic, and then click Apply.

5. Click Start to start the License Logging service.

6. Click OK to close the License Logging Properties dialog box.

7. Close the Services console.

Adding Licenses

1. On the Administrative Tools menu, select Licensing.

2. Select the Products View tab.

    QUESTION   *Are any of the products listed not in compliance with legal licensing requirements?*

3. Click the Windows Server item in the Products view.

4. On the License menu, select New License. The New Client Access License dialog box opens.

5. Make sure that Windows Server is selected in the Product drop-down list.

6. In the Quantity field, type **25**.

7. In the Comments field, type **Issued by *Name***.

8. Click OK. The Per Device Or Per User Licensing dialog box opens.

9. Select the I Agree That check box to indicate that you have purchased CALs for the 25 users who will access the server.

10. Click OK.

    QUESTION   *Is Windows Server compliant with your licensing requirements?*

11. Take a screen capture of the Licensing screen, and save it as C:\Lab Manual \Lab 05\Labwork\Licensing.bmp.

12. Close the Licensing utility.

LAB REVIEW QUESTIONS

Estimated completion time: 10 minutes

1. In your own words, describe what you learned during this lab.

2. What did you have to install on your Windows Server 2003 before you could install Microsoft Software Update Service?

3. What is the purpose of the Microsoft Baseline Security Analyzer?

4. To use the Licensing MMC, what service must you start?

5. You have been asked to create a weekly log of possible security risks on your server. What is the best way to do this?

LAB CHALLENGE 5-1: INSTALLING A MICROSOFT SERVICE PACK

Estimated completion time: 45 minutes

> **NOTE** *Before You Attempt to Install a Service Pack* As of this writing, Microsoft has not yet released SP1 for Windows Server 2003. If your instructor asks you to complete this lab challenge, you will need to obtain the service pack. Either your instructor will provide the service pack or you must download it from the Windows Update Web site.

Microsoft has just released a new service pack for your machines, and you have been asked to install it. Run the install file (Update.exe) to expand the service pack to a directory called C:\Lab Manual\Lab 05\Labwork\NEWSP. After expanding the service pack, run the Setup.exe file in quiet mode.

LAB CHALLENGE 5-2: INSTALLING A MICROSOFT HOTFIX

Estimated completion time: 10 minutes

Microsoft has just released a new hotfix for Internet Explorer, and you have been asked to apply this in your lab before deploying it in your production environment. The hotfix can be found at C:\Lab Manual\Lab 05\Tools\Hotfix\KB824105.exe. If the installation is successful, an entry for the hotfix will appear in Add Or Remove Programs. Take a screenshot of Add Or Remove Programs, and save it as C:\Lab Manual\Lab 05\Labwork\Challenge5-2.bmp.

LAB 6
WORKING WITH USER ACCOUNTS

This lab contains the following exercises and activities:

- Exercise 6-1: Creating an Organizational Unit Structure
- Exercise 6-2: Creating Domain User Accounts
- Exercise 6-3: Adding Information to an Existing Account
- Exercise 6-4: Modifying User Logon Restrictions
- Exercise 6-5: Managing Multiple Users
- Exercise 6-6: Importing User Accounts from a CSV File
- Exercise 6-7: Moving Users
- Exercise 6-8: Creating and Using a Template Account
- Exercise 6-9: Managing User Profiles
- Lab Review Questions
- Lab Challenge 6-1: Using Dsadd.exe and Dsmod.exe

After completing this lab, you will be able to:

- Create and modify user accounts by using the Active Directory Users And Computers MMC snap-in

- Create and modify user accounts by using automation

- Import user accounts

Estimated completion time: 92 minutes

EXERCISE 6-1: CREATING AN ORGANIZATIONAL UNIT STRUCTURE

Estimated completion time: 5 minutes

You have just finished the design of Contoso, Ltd.'s, organizational unit (OU) structure, and you must now create these OUs in your Active Directory. Your design calls for four OUs: Sales, Marketing, Accounts, and Executives.

1. Log on to the computer using your domain Administrator account.

2. Open Active Directory Users And Computers from the Administrative Tools menu.

3. Right-click your domain name (contoso*xx*.com) in the scope pane, point to New, and click Organizational Unit.

   The New Object – Organizational Unit dialog box opens.

4. In the Name field, type **Sales**.

5. Click OK.

6. Repeat these steps to create the remaining three OUs: Marketing, Accounts, and Executives.

EXERCISE 6-2: CREATING DOMAIN USER ACCOUNTS

Estimated completion time: 10 minutes

Human Resources has just sent you a list of new employees who will be joining the company's newly formed Marketing department. You have been asked to create network accounts for these new employees. The company has decided that users should log on using the first character of their first name plus their surname. The new employees' passwords will be given to them on their start dates and will require management's permission to be changed, because company policy requires the use of complex passwords. A complex password is one that contains at least three of the following four elements: uppercase letters, lowercase letters, numbers, and symbols. The new employees are listed in the following table.

First Name	Middle Initial	Last Name
Stephen	Y	Jiang
Brannon		Jones
Frank		Lee
Jeffrey	L	Ford
Maria		Hammond

QUESTION   *What would be the logon name for each of these new users?*

1. Right-click the Marketing OU in the Active Directory Users And Computers scope pane, point to New, and then click User.

   The New Object – User wizard opens.

2. In the First Name text box, type **Stephen**. In the Initials text box, type **Y**. In the Last Name text box, type **Jiang**. In the User Logon Name text box, type the logon name for Stephen Y. Jiang. Click Next.

3. In the Password text box, type **MOAC@LH#1**. In the Confirm Password text box, type **MOAC@LH#1**. Clear the User Must Change Password At Next Logon check box. Select the User Cannot Change Password check box. Click Next.

4. Review the information provided in the New Object – User wizard and click Finish.

5. Repeat steps 1-4 to create accounts for the remaining four users.

EXERCISE 6-3: ADDING INFORMATION TO AN EXISTING ACCOUNT

Estimated completion time: 2 minutes

Maria Hammond has been promoted to Marketing Manager. Human Resources has asked you to add her account to the Account Operators group and to change her title to Marketing Manager.

1. In the Active Directory Users And Computers scope pane, select the Marketing OU.

2. In the details pane, right-click the user account for Maria Hammond, and click Properties. The Maria Hammond Properties dialog box opens.

3. In the Title text box of the Organization tab, type **Marketing Manager**.

4. In the Member Of tab, click Add. The Select Groups dialog box opens.

5. In the Enter Object Names To Select text box, type **Account Operators**.

6. Click OK to close the Select Groups dialog box. The Account Operators group is added to the Member Of list.

7. Click OK to close the Maria Hammond Properties dialog box.

EXERCISE 6-4: MODIFYING USER LOGON RESTRICTIONS

Estimated completion time: 5 minutes

You just received an e-mail from the Human Resources manager instructing you to make sure that Frank Lee is allowed to log on to the network only from 3 A.M. to 5 A.M. on Mondays and Wednesdays, which are his working hours.

1. In the Active Directory Users And Computers scope pane, select the Marketing OU.

2. In the details pane, right-click the user account for Frank Lee, and click Properties. The Frank Lee Properties dialog box opens.

3. Click the Logon Hours button in the Account tab. The Logon Hours For Frank Lee dialog box opens.

4. Select the Logon Denied option.

5. Select the Monday 3 A.M. to 5 A.M. time frame.

   Select the Logon Permitted option. The Logon Hours For Frank Lee dialog box should look like the following:

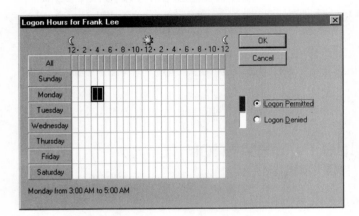

6. Select the Wednesday 3 A.M. to 5 A.M. time frame.

7. Select the Logon Permitted option.

8. Click OK to close the Logon Hours For Frank Lee dialog box.

9. Click OK to close the Frank Lee Properties dialog box.

EXERCISE 6-5: MANAGING MULTIPLE USERS

Estimated completion time: 10 minutes

You need to make a number of changes to all the users in the Marketing OU. The Human Resources Department wants them all to have the Department field set to Marketing and the Description field set to Marketing Personnel.

1. In the Active Directory Users And Computers scope pane, select the Marketing OU.

2. In the details pane, select the account for Brannon Jones, hold down the Shift key, and click the account for Stephen Y. Jiang. All five users in the Marketing OU are selected.

3. Right-click in the highlighted area in the details pane, and click Properties. The Properties On Multiple Objects dialog box appears.

4. In the General tab, select the check box next to Description. The Description text box is enabled.

5. In the Description text box, type **Marketing Personnel**.

6. Select the Organization tab, and select the check box next to Department. The Department text box is enabled.

7. In the Department text box, type **Marketing**.

8. Click OK to close the Properties On Multiple Objects dialog box.

9. Close Active Directory Users And Computers.

EXERCISE 6-6: IMPORTING USER ACCOUNTS FROM A CSV FILE

Estimated completion time: 10 minutes

You have been given a CSV file by the operators of your old computer system. This file contains some new user accounts that need to be imported into your Active Directory. This file has been tested with the old system but has not been tested with Windows Server 2003, so to ensure that any errors in the file are skipped, you will use the -k switch when importing the CSV file.

1. Open Windows Explorer and browse to C:\Lab Manual\Lab 06\Labwork.

2. In the file view, double-click contoso*xx*.csv to open the CSV file. The contoso*xx*.csv file opens in Notepad.

3. You need to edit the CSV file so it is specific to your domain. Replace all occurrences of contoso*xx* (there are 14 in all) with your domain name.

4. On the file menu, select Save As. Save the file using your domain name. For example, if your student number is 01, save the file as contoso01.csv.

5. Close Notepad.

6. Open a command prompt from the Start menu.

7. At the command prompt, type **cd "C:\Lab Manual\Lab 06\Labwork"**, and then press Enter.

8. At the command prompt, type **csvde -i -f contoso*xx*.csv -k**, and then press Enter.

   QUESTION   How many new accounts were added to your Active Directory?

9. At the command prompt, type **Exit**, and then press Enter.

10. Open Active Directory Users And Computers, and select the Accounts OU.

    QUESTION   How many accounts are listed in the Accounts OU?

11. Select the Sales OU.

    QUESTION   How many accounts are listed in the Sales OU?

EXERCISE 6-7: MOVING USERS

Estimated completion time: 10 minutes

Your manager has decided that separate OUs for Sales and Marketing are unnecessary and has asked you to move all the user accounts from Sales into the Marketing OU.

1. In Active Directory Users And Computers, select the Sales OU.

2. Select the account for David Campbell, hold down the Shift key, and click the account for Wendy Kahn. All four accounts in the Sales OU are selected.

3. Right-click any of the selected accounts, and click Move. The Move dialog box opens.

4. In the Move Object Into Container folder tree, select Marketing.

5. Click OK to close the Move dialog box.

6. In Active Directory Users And Computers, select the Marketing OU.

QUESTION   How many accounts are listed in the Marketing OU?

EXERCISE 6-8: CREATING AND USING A TEMPLATE ACCOUNT

Estimated completion time: 15 minutes

You will be creating new accounts in the Executives OU over the next few months. The entire account will have the Department field set to Executives, the Company field set to Contoso, and the Title field set to Company Executives. To simplify your task, you have decided to create a template.

Activity 1: Creating a Template Account

1. Open Active Directory Users And Computers.

2. In the scope pane, browse to the Executives OU.

3. Right-click the Executives OU, point to New, and then click User. The New Object – User wizard opens.

4. In the First Name text box, type **Executives**.

5. In the Last Name text box, type **Template**.

6. In the Full Name text box, type an underscore at the beginning of Executives Template (to read _Executives Template).

7. In the User Logon Name text box, type **Executives**.

8. Click Next.

9. In the Password text box, type **MOAC@LH#1**.

10. In the Confirm Password text box, type **MOAC@LH#1**.

11. Clear the User Must Change Password At Next Logon check box.

12. Select the User Cannot Change Password check box.

13. Select the Account Is Disabled check box.

14. Click Next.

15. Review the information in the summary page of the New Object – User wizard, and click Finish.

QUESTION   Why do you think we placed an underscore at the beginning of the Executives Template Full Name?

16. Right-click the _Executives Template account in the details pane, and click Properties. The _Executives Template Properties dialog box opens.

17. Select the Organization tab.

18. In the Title text box, type **Company Executives**.

19. In the Department text box, type **Executives**.

20. In the Company text box, type **Contoso**.

21. Click OK to close the _Executives Template Properties dialog box.

Activity 2: Using the Template Account

Use the template account to create a new user account in the Executives OU.

1. Right-click on the _Executives Template account in the details pane, and click Copy. The Copy Object – User wizard opens.

2. In the First Name text box, type **Eric**.

3. In the Last Name text box, type **Parkinson**.

4. In the User Logon Name text box, type **eparkinson**.

5. Click Next.

   QUESTION   Why is the Account Is Disabled check box selected?

6. In the Password text box, type **MOAC@LH#1**.

7. In the Confirm Password text box, type **MOAC@LH#1**.

8. Clear the Account Is Disabled check box.

9. Click Next.

10. Review the information in the summary page of the New Object – User wizard, and click Finish.

11. In the Active Directory Users And Computers details pane, right-click the account for Eric Parkinson, and click Properties. The Eric Parkinson Properties dialog box opens.

12. Select the Organization tab.

   QUESTION   Have the three properties (Title, Company, and Department) we set on the Executives Template account been copied over to this new account?

13. Click OK to close the Eric Parkinson Properties dialog box.

EXERCISE 6-9: MANAGING USER PROFILES

Estimated completion time: 20 minutes

Many of the users in the company share machines, so you are looking into how their desktop settings are saved and how to make it easier for users when they move to different machines.

1. Open Windows Explorer and browse to the C:\Documents And Settings directory.

QUESTION   What directories are listed below the Documents And Settings directory?

2. Close all open windows and applications.

3. Log off your machine.

4. Log on as Maria Hamond (mhammond), using the password MOAC@LH#1.

5. Log off the machine.

6. Log on as Administrator using the password MOAC@LH#1.

7. Open Windows Explorer, and browse to the C:\Documents And Settings directory.

QUESTION   What directories are listed below the Documents And Settings directory?

8. Log off the machine.

9. Log on as Maria Hammond (mhammond) using the password MOAC@LH#1.

10. Right-click on your desktop, and click Properties. The Display Properties dialog box opens.

11. Select the Desktop tab.

12. From the Backgrounds list, select Friend.

13. Click OK. You should see that the background of the desktop has changed.

14. Log off the machine.

15. Log on as Administrator using your password.

QUESTION   Has the Administrator's desktop changed? Why or why not?

LAB REVIEW QUESTIONS

1. What benefit do you gain by creating Account templates?

2. What is the purpose of the -k switch when you use CSVDE?

3. You need to move a user account from one OU to another. What steps do you take?

4. What is a complex password?

LAB CHALLENGE 6-1: USING DSADD.EXE AND DSMOD.EXE

Estimated completion time: 25 minutes

You have been asked to investigate the use of Dsadd and Dsmod to manage user accounts on your network. You will create a new user in the Sales OU named David So. David's logon name will be dso, and his display name will be David So.

Sample Procedure for Lab Challenge 1: Using Dsadd.exe and Dsmod.exe

1. Open a command prompt and type the following (where *xx* is your computer number):

   ```
   dsadd user "CN=David So,OU=Sales,DC=Contosoxx,DC=com" -samid dso -ln
     So -fn David -upn dso@contosoxx.com
   ```

2. Press Enter.

3. Having created an account for David So in Active Directory using Dsadd, you want to change his Description to Sales Manager. Type the following at the command prompt (where *xx* is your computer number).

   ```
   dsmod user "CN=David So,OU=Sales,DC=Contosoxx,DC=com" -desc "Sales Manager"
   ```

4. Press Enter.

5. Open Active Directory Users And Computers, and verify that the account for David So has been created and that the Description property is set to Sales Manager.

6. You now need to create another user named Wendy Wheeler in the Marketing OU. The Description property should be set to Marketing Executive, the Department property set to Marketing, and the Company property set to Contoso. Her password needs to be set to MOAC@LM#1, and her account needs to be enabled.

   QUESTION   Write down the command line you would use to perform this task.

7. Open a command prompt, and create the user named Wendy Wheeler using the command you just wrote.

8. Take a screen capture showing the account in Active Directory Users And Computers to verify that the account has been created. Save the screen capture as C:\Lab Manual\Lab 06\Labwork\Challenge6-1.bmp.

REVIEWING YOUR ENVIRONMENT

You are one of the network administrators for Contoso Pharmaceuticals. The company network consists of a single Active Directory domain named contoso*xx*.com (where *xx* is your assigned student number). Microsoft Windows Server 2003 was installed by a consultant and has been running for about three months without any issues. The company has decided to have user accounts grouped by job function, so if you work in the company's Sales department, for example, your user account will be placed in the Sales OU in Active Directory.

You are responsible for carrying out some day-to-day maintenance of user accounts and ensuring that critical data is backed up daily and that you can recover any missing data. As a senior member of the IT team, you also have some additional responsibilities, including monitoring servers for errors, ensuring that the servers meet the company's performance expectations, keeping the servers up to date with security patches and hotfixes, monitoring the company's Client Access Licenses (CALs) to ensure that Contoso is not running more clients than it owns licenses for, and monitoring the servers for security vulnerabilities.

Contoso Pharmaceuticals has just implemented a user account and password policy, which you must adhere to. The policy is as follows:

- Users must log on to the network using the first character of their first name followed by their full last name.

- Each user must be given a default password of MOAC@LH#1, and they are not allowed to change this password.

- Junior administrators must be placed in the Account Operators group, not the Administrator group.

- Users must be placed into an OU that corresponds to their department or job function:

Department or Job Function	OU
Sales	Sales
Marketing	Marketing
IT	IT
Junior administrator	IT\Junior Admins
Accounts	Accounting

Based on the information provided, answer the following questions:

1. Tai Yee has just been hired as a junior administrator for Contoso Pharmaceuticals. What should Tai's logon name be?

2. What OU should you create Tai's account in?

3. What group should Tai's account be placed in?

4. What tool do you use to create Tai's account?

5. You are responsible for ensuring that Contoso's servers are running properly. You want to be notified if the hard disk space on one of your drives falls below 250 MB. What tool and what feature of that tool do you use?

6. When one of your servers reboots, it reports that an error occurred while booting. You can click OK and continue to log on. What tool do you use to see what errors were generated during the reboot?

7. Keeping up to date with hotfixes and security patches has become a large job. You visit each workstation daily and apply hotfixes manually from a network share. You have been asked to find a more efficient way of managing hotfixes and security patches. What Microsoft tool can assist you with hotfix and security patch management?

8. What must you back up to ensure that Active Directory and all other critical components of the server have been backed up?

9. You are assisting a user with a problem on her Windows XP machine when a manager calls to ask you to check the event log on one of your servers. The manager is in a meeting and needs the information right away. What tool do you use, and how would you run it?

10. Contoso was recently audited by a regulatory agency that oversees the pharmaceutical industry, and you were unable to provide a complete list of all the software licenses that Contoso holds. Your manager has asked you to find a way of keeping track of all the company's software licenses so this information will be readily available. What feature of Windows Server 2003 can you use for this purpose?

LAB DEPENDENCIES

To complete this lab, you must have the following:

- A machine that is running Windows Server 2003 and Active Directory. (Lab Exercises 1-1 and 1-2 cover the installation of Windows Server 2003.)

- A user account for Maria Hammond, which has been added to the Account Operators group. This account was created in Lab Exercise 6-2 and added to the Account Operators group in Lab Exercise 6-3.

CHANGING THE COMPUTER CONFIGURATION

In this portion of the lab, you or your instructor will change the computer configuration to facilitate troubleshooting in the following section. Two break scenarios are presented in this section. Your instructor will decide which computers will be subject to which break scenarios.

TROUBLESHOOTING

In this portion of the lab, you must resolve a number of configuration issues created in the "Changing the Computer Configuration" section.

As you resolve the issues, fill out a Troubleshooting Lab Worksheet (found at C:\Lab Manual\TroubleshootingLabA\Worksheet.doc) and include the following information:

- Description of the issue.
- A list of all steps taken to attempt to diagnose the problem.
- What was the problem?
- What was the solution?
- A list of resources you used to solve the problem.

Break Scenario 1

You are a senior network administrator for Contoso Pharmaceuticals, and the user named Maria Hammond has called you about a Remote Desktop issue. Maria often works out of the office. She needs to be able to connect to the Server*xx* server remotely using the Remote Desktop tool, but is having problems connecting to this server. She is currently away from the office, so she cannot say exactly what error message she has received.

Maria has also asked you to investigate a problem that she experienced a few days ago when she was still able to log on to the network. Somebody created a customized MMC for her so that she could use the Event Viewer. The last time she used it she was unable to see any entries in the Application log, but she could see entries in the other log files, and would like you to investigate this after resolving her logon problem.

Break Scenario 2

You are a senior network administrator for Contoso Pharmaceuticals. The user named Maria Hammond calls to inform you that an important file is missing from the HR Documents directory on the server. The file that is missing is called HR Report2.txt, and she needs this file recovered as soon as possible. You check your backup logs and notice that the HR Documents directory (C:\Lab Manual \TroubleshootingLabA\HR Documents) was backed up last night to the C:\Lab Manual\TroubleshootingLabA\HR Documents Backup directory.

All the users on your network have reported that they are unable to connect to the server using Remote Desktop. You must diagnose the problem and solve it.

LAB 7
WORKING WITH GROUPS

This lab contains the following exercises and activities:

- Exercise 7-1: Raising the Functional Level of Your Domain
- Exercise 7-2: Creating Global Security Groups
- Exercise 7-3: Creating Domain Local Security Groups
- Exercise 7-4: Creating Groups Using Dsadd
- Exercise 7-5: Adding Members to the Group
- Exercise 7-6: Adding Global Groups to Domain Local Groups
- Exercise 7-7: Using Dsget to Find Group Memberships
- Lab Review Questions
- Lab Challenge 7-1: Changing the Scope of a Group
- Lab Challenge 7-2: Using Dsmod to Add Members to a Group

LAB DEPENDENCIES

In order to complete this lab, you must be sure that the following is done:

- Exercises from Lab 1 are completed
- Exercises from Lab 6 are completed

After completing this lab, you will be able to:

- Raise the functional level of a domain
- Identify and modify the scope of a group
- Find domain groups in which a user is a member
- Manage group membership
- Create and modify groups by using Active Directory Users And Computers
- Create and modify groups by using automation

Estimated completion time: 100 minutes

EXERCISE 7-1: RAISING THE FUNCTIONAL LEVEL OF YOUR DOMAIN

Estimated completion time: 5 minutes

All of the domain controllers on your network have been upgraded to Windows Server 2003, so you have been asked to raise the functional level of your domain from the default Windows 2000 mixed functional level to the Windows Server 2003 functional level.

1. Log on to your domain as Administrator.

2. On the Administrative Tools menu, select Active Directory Domains And Trusts. The Active Directory Domains and Trusts console opens.

3. Right-click your domain name (contoso*xx*.com), and select Raise Domain Functional Level. The Raise Domain Functional Level dialog box opens:

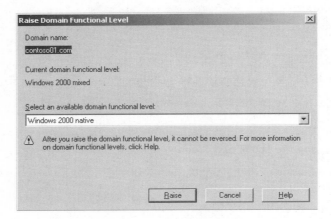

4. Select Windows Server 2003 from the Select An Available Domain Functional Level drop-down list.

5. Click Raise. The following message box is displayed:

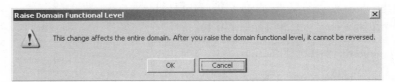

6. Click OK to confirm the raising of the domain functional level. A message box appears, informing you that you have raised your domain functional level successfully.

7. Click OK.

8. Close the Active Directory Domains and Trusts console.

EXERCISE 7-2: CREATING GLOBAL SECURITY GROUPS

Estimated completion time: 10 minutes

After carefully planning your organization's group requirements, you have been asked to create three global security groups, one for marketing personnel (Marketing Personnel), one for marketing executives (Marketing

Executives), and one that includes all members of the Marketing department (All Marketing).

1. Open Active Directory Users and Computers.

2. Right-click the Marketing OU in the scope pane, point to New, and select Group. The New Object - Group dialog box opens:

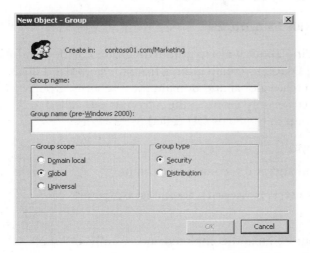

3. In the Group Name text box, type **Marketing Personnel**. Leave the defaults for all other settings, and click OK.

4. Repeat steps 2 and 3 to create the Marketing Executives and All Marketing global security groups.

5. When you have created all three groups, take a screen capture of the Active Directory Users and Computers console, ensuring that all three groups in the Marketing OU are visible. Save the screen capture as C:\Lab Manual\Lab 07\Labwork\Exercise7-2.bmp.

EXERCISE 7-3: CREATING DOMAIN LOCAL SECURITY GROUPS

Estimated completion time: 10 minutes

To help secure access to resources on your network, you must create some domain local security groups for the Marketing department and create two domain local security groups, one called Marketing Readers and one called Marketing Full Control.

1. In Active Directory Users and Computers, right-click the Marketing OU, point to New, and select Group. The New Object - Group dialog box opens.

2. In the Group Name text box, type **Marketing Readers**.

3. In the Group Scope section, select the Domain Local option.

4. Leave all other options as the default, and click OK.

5. Repeat steps 2 through 4 to create the Marketing Full Control group.

6. When you have created both of the domain local security groups, take a screen capture of Active Directory Users and Computers console, ensuring that both groups in the Marketing OU are visible. Save the screen capture as C:\Lab Manual\Lab 07\Labwork\Exercise7-3.bmp.

EXERCISE 7-4: CREATING GROUPS USING DSADD

Estimated completion time: 15 minutes

Your manager has been reading about ways to automate group creation and has asked you to look into using Dsadd to create groups from the command line. She wants you to see if you can create global and domain local security groups with Dsadd. You will create a global security group in the Accounts OU called Accounts Users and a domain local group in the Sales OU called Sales Users.

1. Open a command prompt.

2. Enter the following command at the command prompt:

   `dsadd group "cn=Accounts Users,ou=Accounts,dc=contosoxx,dc=com"`

3. Press ENTER.

4. You are notified that your command completed successfully and the group was created, as shown here:

5. Close the command prompt.

6. In Active Directory Users and Computers, navigate to the Accounts OU.

   QUESTION What is the scope and type (found in the Type column) of the Accounts Users group?

7. Open a command prompt, and type the following command:

   `dsadd group "cn=Sales Users,ou=Sales,dc=contosoxx,dc=com"`
   `   -scope l -secgrp yes`

8. Press ENTER.

9. You are notified that your command completed successfully and the group was created, as shown here:

10. Close the command prompt.

11. In Active Directory Users and Computers, navigate to the Sales OU.

> **QUESTION**   What is the scope and type of the Sales User group?

12. Close Active Directory Users and Computers.

EXERCISE 7-5: ADDING MEMBERS TO THE GROUP

Estimated completion time: 20 minutes

Human Resources has given you a list of users, along with the group that you should put them into. Some of the users will be placed in the Marketing Executives global group, and some will be placed in the Marketing Personnel global group, as shown in the following table.

Group	Members
Marketing Executives	Wendy Wheeler
	Deb Waldal
	David Campbell
	Wendy Kahn
Marketing Personnel	Brannon Jones
	Stephen Y. Jiang
	Jeffrey L. Ford
	Maria Hammond
	Frank Lee

1. Open Active Directory Users and Computers, and click the Marketing OU.

2. Click Wendy Wheeler, hold down the CTRL key, and click on each user who should be a member of the Marketing Executives group.

3. Right-click one of the selected users, and select Add To Group. The Select Group dialog box opens:

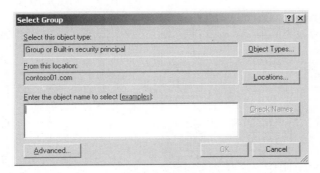

4. In the Enter The Object Name To Select text box, type **Marketing Executives**.

5. Click Check Names. Marketing Executives will appear underlined.

6. Click OK to close the Select Group dialog box. A message box appears, indicating that you have successfully added the users to the group:

7. Click OK to close the message box.

8. Right-click the Marketing Executives group in the details pane, and select Properties. The Marketing Executives Properties dialog box opens.

9. Select the Members tab. You should see the four members listed. Take a screen capture, and save it as C:\Lab Manual\Lab 07\Labwork\Exercise7-5a.bmp.

10. Click OK to close the Marketing Executives Properties dialog box.

11. Right-click the Marketing Personnel group in the details pane, and select Properties. The Marketing Personnel Properties dialog box opens.

12. Select the Members tab. Notice that this group does not contain any members at present.

13. Click Add. The Select Users, Contacts, Computers, Or Groups dialog box opens:

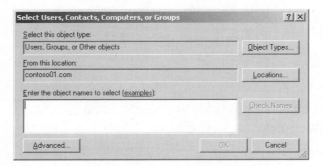

14. In the Enter The Object Name To Select text box, type **Brannon Jones; Stephen Y. Jiang; Jeffrey L. Ford; Maria Hammond; Frank Lee**. Click Check Names. The names will appear underlined, as shown here:

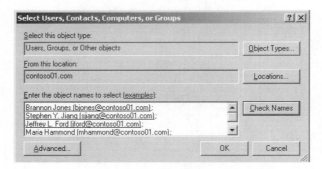

15. Click OK to close the Select Users, Contacts, Computers, Or Groups dialog box. Five members are listed in the Members tab of the Marketing Personnel Properties dialog box.

16. Take a screenshot of this dialog box, and save it as C:\Lab Manual\Lab 07 \Labwork\Exercise7-5b.bmp.

17. Click OK to close the Marketing Personnel Properties dialog box.

18. Close Active Directory Users and Computers.

EXERCISE 7-6: ADDING GLOBAL GROUPS TO DOMAIN LOCAL GROUPS

Estimated completion time: 10 minutes

To make group management easier, you will add the Marketing Executives global group to the Marketing Full Control domain local group and then add the Marketing Personnel global group to the Marketing Readers domain local group.

1. Open Active Directory Users and Computers.

2. Select the Marketing OU.

3. Right-click the Marketing Full Control group in the details pane, and select Properties. The Marketing Full Control Properties dialog box opens.

4. Select the Members tab. Notice that there are no members of this group.

5. Click Add. The Select Users, Contacts, Computers Or Groups dialog box opens.

6. In the Enter The Object Names To Select text box, type **Marketing Executives**, and then click Check Names. The Marketing Executives group appears underlined.

7. Click OK to close the Select Users, Contacts, Computers Or Groups dialog box. The Marketing Executives group appears in the Members tab for the Marketing Full Control domain local group:

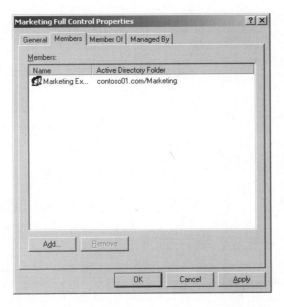

8. Click OK to close the Marketing Full Control Properties dialog box.

9. Right-click the Marketing Executives group in the details pane, and select Properties. The Marketing Executives Properties dialog box opens.

10. Select the Member Of tab.

    QUESTION *Of what groups is the Marketing Executives group a member?*

11. Click OK to close the Marketing Executives Properties dialog box.

12. Repeat the steps above to add the Marketing Personnel global group to the Marketing Readers domain local group.

13. Take a screen capture of the Member Of tab for the Marketing Personnel group, and save it as C:\Lab Manual\Lab 07\Labwork\Exercise7-6.bmp.

14. Close Active Directory Users and Computers.

EXERCISE 7-7: USING DSGET TO FIND GROUP MEMBERSHIPS

Estimated completion time: 5 minutes

You have been asked to locate the groups that Maria Hammond is a member of. You do not currently have access to the Active Directory Users and Computers, so you must use a command-line utility to do the job.

1. Open a command prompt, and enter the following:

```
dsget user "cn=Maria Hammond, ou=Marketing, dc=contosoxx, dc=com"
    -memberof
```

2. Press ENTER.

    QUESTION *What groups does Maria Hammond currently belong to?*

LAB REVIEW QUESTIONS

Estimated completion time: 10 minutes

1. What is the benefit of using Dsadd to create groups instead of using Active Directory Users and Computers?

2. What are three ways that you can add members to a group?

3. What command-line utility do you use to get a list of groups that the administrator account is a member of? Give an example of the syntax.

4. What administrative tool do you use to raise the functional level of your domain?

5. What were the scopes of the groups that you created during this lab?

LAB CHALLENGE 7-1: CHANGING THE SCOPE OF A GROUP

Estimated completion time: 5 minutes

When the All Marketing group was created, it was created as a Global group. However, it should have been created as a universal group. After changing the scope of the group, take a screen capture of the Marketing OU in Active Directory Users and Computers, showing that the All Marketing group is now a universal group. Save the screen capture as C:\Lab Manual\Lab 07\Labwork\Challenge7-1.bmp.

LAB CHALLENGE 7-2: USING DSMOD TO ADD MEMBERS TO A GROUP

Estimated completion time: 10 minutes

You have been instructed to add the Marketing Executives and Marketing Personnel groups to the All Marketing universal group. You must do this using the Dsmod command-line utility.

1. What is the syntax for adding the Marketing Executives and Marketing Personnel groups to the All Marketing universal group?

2. Run the Dsmod command from the command prompt using the syntax that you listed above. If it is successful, take a screen capture of the result and save it as C:\Lab Manual\Lab 07\Labwork\Challenge7-2a.bmp.

3. Using Active Directory Users and Computers, open the properties for the All Marketing group and select the Members tab. Take a screen capture showing the two groups that are listed, and save it as C:\Lab Manual\Lab 07\Labwork\Challenge7-2b.bmp.

WORKING WITH COMPUTER ACCOUNTS

This lab contains the following exercises and activities:

■ Exercise 8-1: Creating Computer Accounts Using Active Directory Users and Computers

■ Exercise 8-2: Creating Computer Accounts Using Dsadd

■ Exercise 8-3: Deleting, Disabling, and Resetting Computer Accounts

■ Lab Review Questions

■ Lab Challenge 8-1: Changing the Properties of Computer Accounts

After completing this lab, you will be able to:

■ Create and manage computer accounts in an Active Directory environment

■ Reset computer accounts

Estimated completion time: 45 minutes

EXERCISE 8-1: CREATING COMPUTER ACCOUNTS USING ACTIVE DIRECTORY USERS AND COMPUTERS

Estimated completion time: 10 minutes

Your manager has asked you to create five new computer accounts in Active Directory for some new workstations that will be installed on the company network. The names of these new computers will be WORKSTATION01 through WORKSTATION05, and they must be created in the Computers container in Active Directory.

1. Log on as Administrator.

2. Open Active Directory Users and Computers.

3. Right-click the Computers container in the scope pane, point to New, and select Computer.

   The New Object – Computer wizard appears, as shown here:

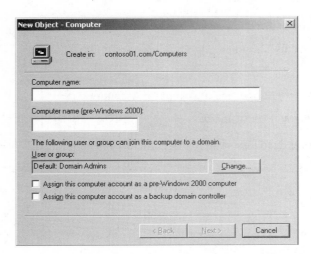

4. In the Computer Name text box, type **WORKSTATION01**.

5. Leave the remaining fields with their defaults and click Next.

   The Managed page of the wizard opens.

6. Leave the default settings, and click Next.

   The summary page of the New Object – Computer wizard appears.

7. Click Finish to close the wizard.

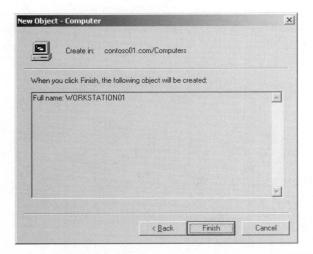

8. Repeat steps 3 through 7 to create the remaining four workstation accounts.

9. Take a screen capture of the Computer container in Active Directory Users and Computers, showing the five workstation accounts. Save the screen capture as C:\Lab Manual\Lab 08\Labwork\Exercise8-1.bmp.

10. Close Active Directory Users and Computers.

EXERCISE 8-2: CREATING COMPUTER ACCOUNTS USING DSADD

Estimated completion time: 10 minutes

In the coming months, the company will be adding a large number of workstations to its network, and your manager has asked you to look at how to use Dsadd to possibly automate the process. You will need to create accounts for WORKSTATION06 through WORKSTATION08.

1. Open a command prompt, and type **dsadd computer "cn=WORKSTATION06,cn=Computers,dc=contoso*xx*,dc=com"**.

2. Press ENTER. You receive notification that your command was completed successfully, as shown here:

3. Repeat steps 1 and 2 for WORKSTATION07 and WORKSTATION08.

4. Open Active Directory Users and Computers, and navigate to the Computers container.

5. Take a screen capture of the Computers container, showing the eight computer accounts, and save it as C:\Lab Manual\Lab 08\Labwork\Exercise8-2.bmp.

EXERCISE 8-3: DELETING, DISABLING, AND RESETTING COMPUTER ACCOUNTS

Estimated completion time: 10 minutes

Management has decided that WORKSTATION01 will not be used for a few weeks, so for security reasons you must disable its account. WORKSTATION02 was previously used, but a new machine will use the name WORKSTATION02 so you must reset the account so the new machine can join the domain. WORKSTATION08 will not be used on the network, so you must delete its account from Active Directory.

1. In Active Directory Users and Computers, select the Computers container.

2. Right-click WORKSTATION01 in the details pane, and select Disable Account.

An Active Directory message box appears, indicating that users can no longer log on from this machine, as shown here:

3. Click Yes. You are notified that the account has been disabled.

4. Click OK. Notice that the icon for WORKSTATION01 now has a red X next to it, indicating that it is disabled.

5. Right-click WORKSTATION02, and select Reset Account.

   An Active Directory message box appears, asking you to confirm the resetting of this account, as shown here:

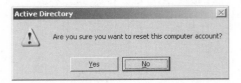

6. Click Yes.

   A message box appears, indicating that the account has been successfully reset.

7. Click OK.

8. Right-click WORKSTATION08, and select Delete.

   A message box appears, asking you to confirm the deletion of the object.

9. Click Yes.

   WORKSTATION08 is deleted from Active Directory.

10. Take a screen capture of Active Directory Users and Computers showing the Computers container, and save it as C:\Lab Manual\Lab 08\Labwork \Exercise8-3.bmp.

LAB REVIEW QUESTIONS

Estimated completion time: 5 minutes

1. Can a user whose account is enabled log on from a workstation whose account is disabled?

2. List two ways that you can create Computer accounts in Active Directory.

3. You have a machine on your network that was rebuilt after its hard disk failed. When you try to join the workstation to the domain, you receive an error message. How you do solve this problem?

4. You have to install a new workstation for a user. While you are at her desk working on joining the workstation to the domain, you remember that you did not create an account in Active Directory for this machine. Is it still possible to join this workstation to the domain without first creating an account for it in Active Directory?

LAB CHALLENGE 8-1: CHANGING THE PROPERTIES OF COMPUTER ACCOUNTS

Estimated completion time: 10 minutes

Management is keen on using the Active Directory search feature to locate resources on the network based on description, so you must populate the description field for all the workstations. WORKSTATION01 through WORKSTATION04 are laptops, and WORKSTATION05 through WORKSTATION07 are desktop machines.

LAB 9
SHARING FILE SYSTEM RESOURCES

This lab contains the following exercises and activities:

- Exercise 9-1: Creating a Shared Folder
- Exercise 9-2: Viewing the NTFS and Share Permissions on a Directory
- Exercise 9-3: Connecting to the Share from the Run Command and Mapping a Drive to the Share
- Exercise 9-4: Setting Share Permissions
- Exercise 9-5: Setting NTFS Permissions
- Exercise 9-6: Viewing Effective Permissions
- Exercise 9-7: Disabling Anonymous Access on the Default Web Site
- Exercise 9-8: Taking Ownership of a File
- Lab Review Questions
- Lab Challenge 9-1: Adding a File to the Company Intranet and Setting Permissions

LAB DEPENDENCIES

To complete this lab, you must be sure that you have done the following:

- Completed Lab Exercise 5-3 to install IIS on your computer
- Completed all Lab 6 Exercises
- Completed all Lab 7 Exercises

After completing this lab, you will be able to:

■ **Manage shared folder permissions**

■ **Verify effective permissions when granting permissions**

■ **Change ownership of files and folders**

■ **Troubleshoot access to files and shared folders**

■ **Manage security for Microsoft Internet Information Services (IIS)**

Estimated completion time: 135 minutes

EXERCISE 9-1: CREATING A SHARED FOLDER

Estimated completion time: 10 minutes

You have been asked by your manager to create a directory called Accounting Data on the C drive of your server. This folder will be used by certain members of the Accounting department to store sensitive company data.

1. Log on as Administrator.

2. Open Windows Explorer from the Start menu, and browse to your C drive.

3. Right-click a blank area in the file view, point to New, and select Folder.

   A new folder is created with the default name New Folder.

4. In the Folder Name text box, type **Accounting Data**, and hit ENTER.

   The new folder is displayed with the name Accounting Data.

5. Right-click Accounting Data, and select Sharing And Security to open the Accounting Data Properties dialog box.

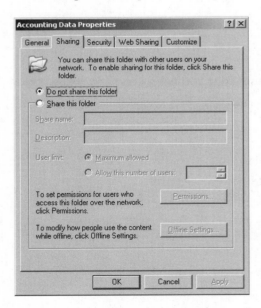

6. Select the Share This Folder option.

7. In the Share Name text box, type **Accounting**.

8. In the Description field, type **Corp Accounting Data**.

9. Click OK to close the Accounting Data Properties dialog box.

   QUESTION   *What indication do you get from the Windows Explorer file view that the Accounting Data directory is now shared?*

EXERCISE 9-2: VIEWING THE NTFS AND SHARE PERMISSIONS ON A DIRECTORY

Estimated completion time: 10 minutes

Because of corporate policy, you have been asked to document the default NTFS and Share permissions assigned to the Accounting Data directory.

1. Right-click the Accounting Data folder in Windows Explorer, and select Sharing And Security.

   The Accounting Data Properties dialog box opens.

2. Select the Security tab.

   QUESTION   *List the groups or users that have permissions for this directory. What standard permissions does each group or user have?*

3. Select the Sharing tab, which shows the sharing properties for the Accounting Data directory.

4. Click Permissions.

   QUESTION   *What are the default Share permissions for the Accounting Data directory?*

5. Click OK twice to close the Accounting Data Properties dialog box.

6. Close Windows Explorer.

EXERCISE 9-3: CONNECTING TO THE SHARE FROM THE RUN COMMAND AND MAPPING A DRIVE TO THE SHARE

Estimated completion time: 10 minutes

You have just created a share for your Accounts department, and you want to create a drive mapping on your server for the share. You plan to map the share to drive X to make it easier for you to work with the information in the share.

1. On the Start menu, click Run.

   The Run dialog box is displayed.

2. In the Open text box, type **Serverxx** and click OK.

   Windows Explorer opens, presenting a list of the shares on your machine.

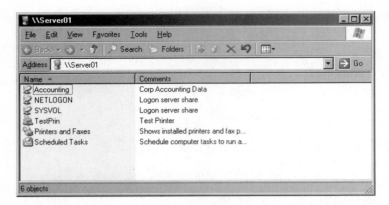

3. Right-click the Accounting share that you created in Exercise 9-1, and select Map Network Drive.

The Map Network Drive dialog box appears.

4. In the Drive drop-down list, select X:.

5. Click Finish.

6. The X drive opens on your machine. Close this window.

7. Close the \\Server*xx* window.

8. On the Start menu, click My Computer.

The My Computer window is displayed.

9. Double-click the line that divides the Name and Type columns to expand the Name field.

10. Take a screen capture of the My Computer window, and save it as C:\Lab Manual\Lab 09\Labwork\Exercise9-3.bmp.

11. Close the My Computer window.

EXERCISE 9-4: SETTING SHARE PERMISSIONS

Estimated completion time: 25 minutes

You have been asked by your manager to assign permissions to the Accounting Data share so that only Administrators can write information into it until the Human Resources department confirms that the user accounts have been established correctly.

1. On the Start menu, click My Computer.

   The My Computer window opens.

2. Double-click the Accounting On 'Server*xx*' (X:) network drive to open the X:\ window.

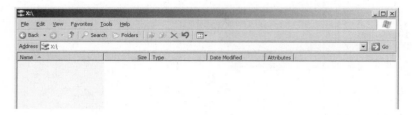

3. Right-click in the blank area, point to New, and select Text Document.

   QUESTION   What is the text in the message box that is displayed when you try creating the new file?

   QUESTION   Why does this message appear?

4. Click OK to close the message box.

5. Close the X: window.

6. Open Windows Explorer and browse to the C drive.

7. Right-click the Accounting Data folder and select Properties.

   The Accounting Data Properties dialog box is displayed.

8. Select the Sharing tab, which shows the sharing properties for the Accounting Data directory.

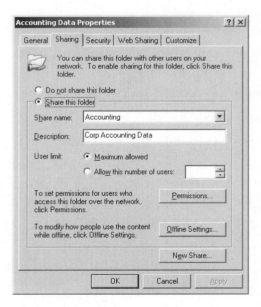

9. Click Permissions to open the Permissions For Accounting dialog box, which shows the permissions for the Accounting share.

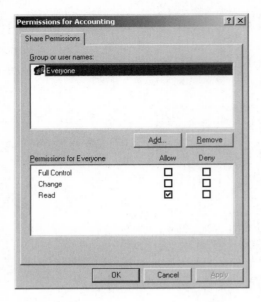

10. Click Add.

    The Select Users, Computers, Or Groups dialog box opens.

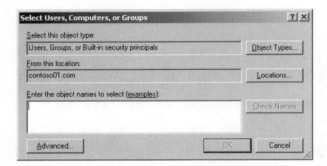

11. In the Enter The Object Names To Select text box, type **Administrators** and click OK.

    The Administrators group appears in the permissions list.

12. Select Administrators in the Group Or User Names list box.

13. Select the Allow check box next to Full Control in the Permissions For Administrators list box.

14. Take a screen capture of this dialog box and save it as C:\Lab Manual \Lab 09\Labwork\Exercise9-4a.bmp.

15. Click OK to close the Permissions For Accounting dialog box.

16. Click OK to close the Accounting Data Properties dialog box.

17. Close Windows Explorer.

18. On the Start menu, click My Computer.

    The My Computer window opens.

19. Double-click the Accounting On 'Server*xx*' (X:) network drive to open the X:\ window.

20. Right-click in the blank area, point to New, and select Text Document.

> **QUESTION**   *Where you able to successfully create a new document in the*
> *X network drive?*

21. Right-click the new text document and select Rename.

22. Rename the document as *YourName*.txt.

23. Take a screen capture of the X:\ window and save it as C:\Lab Manual
\Lab 09\Labwork\Exercise9-4b.bmp.

24. Close the X:\ window.

EXERCISE 9-5: SETTING NTFS PERMISSIONS

Estimated completion time: 25 minutes

You have received approval from the Human Resources department to allow one
of the Marketing executives and three new members of the Accounts department
access to the accounting data. You want to add these users in the simplest manner
possible to allow for ease of administration. The accounts of the three new
members are all currently disabled, so you must also enable their accounts.

1. On the Administrative Tools menu, click Active Directory Users And Computers.

2. Select the Accounts OU in the scope pane.

The members of the Accounts OU are displayed in the details pane.

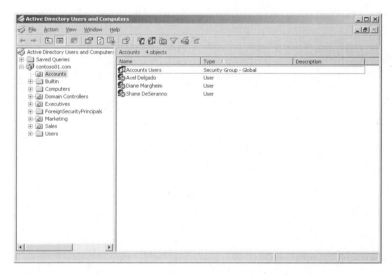

3. Click Axel Delgado, hold down the SHIFT key, and click Shane DeSeranno.

The three user accounts are highlighted.

4. On the Action menu, click Enable Account.

A dialog box confirming that the accounts have been successfully enabled
is displayed.

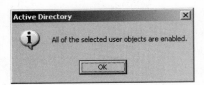

5. Click OK.

6. Make sure the three user accounts are still highlighted. On the Action menu, click Add To A Group.

   The Select Group dialog box opens.

7. In the Enter The Object Name To Select text box, type **Accounts Users**.

8. Click OK.

   A dialog box confirming that the accounts have been successfully added to the group appears.

9. Click OK.

10. Select the Marketing OU in the scope pane.

    The members of the Marketing OU are displayed in the details pane.

11. Right-click the Maria Hammond account, point to All Tasks, and select Add To A Group.

    The Select Group dialog box opens.

12. Repeat steps 7–9 to add Maria Hammond to the Accounts Users group.

13. Close Active Directory Users And Computers.

14. Open Windows Explorer and browse to the C drive.

15. Right-click Accounting Data and select Properties.

    The Accounting Data Properties dialog box opens.

16. Select the Security tab, which displays the current security settings for the Accounting Data directory.

17. Click Add.

    The Select Users, Computers Or Groups dialog box opens.

18. In the Enter The Object Names To Select text box, type **Accounts Users**.

19. Click OK to close the Select Users, Computers Or Groups dialog box.

20. Select the entry for the Accounts Users group and grant the group the Allow Modify permission.

21. Take a screen capture of your security settings and save it as C:\Lab Manual \Lab 09\Labwork\Exercise9-5a.bmp.

22. Select the Sharing tab, which shows the sharing properties for the Accounting Data directory.

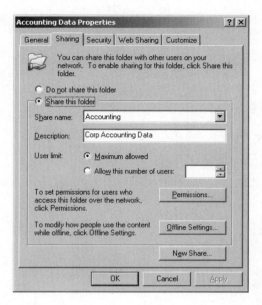

23. Click Permissions to display the share permissions for the Accounting share.

24. Select the Everyone special identity and grant it the Allow Full Control share permission.

25. Click OK twice.

26. Log off your machine.

27. Log on as Maria Hammond (mhammond). Her password is **MOAC@LH#1**.

28. Open the Run dialog box from the Start menu, type **\\Server*xx*** in the Open text box, and click OK.

    Windows Explorer opens, displaying a list of the shares available on your machine.

29. Double-click the Accounting share to show its contents.

30. Right-click in the blank area, point to New, and select Text Document.

31. Name the text document Maria Hammond.txt.

32. Take a screen capture of Windows Explorer showing the Accounting share, and save it as C:\Lab Manual\Lab 09\Labwork\Exercise9-5b.bmp.

33. Close all windows and log off.

EXERCISE 9-6: VIEWING EFFECTIVE PERMISSIONS

Estimated completion time: 10 minutes

You have received a call from a member of your help desk who is working on a problem with Axel Delgado. Axel is having problems saving files, and the help desk wants to know what Axel's effective permissions are on the Accounting Data folder.

1. Log on as Administrator.

2. Open Windows Explorer and browse to your C drive.

3. Right-click Accounting Data and select Properties.

4. Select the Security tab, which shows the security properties for the Accounting Data directory.

5. Click Advanced to open the Advanced Security Settings For Accounting Data dialog box.

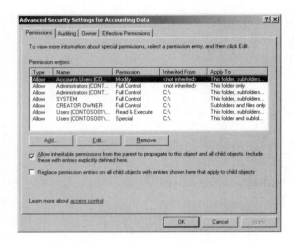

6. Select the Effective Permissions tab.

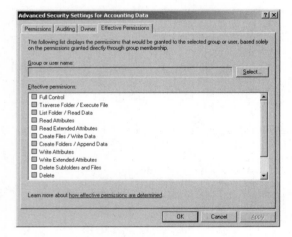

7. Click Select.

   The Select Users, Computers Or Groups dialog box opens.

8. In the Enter The Object Name To Select text box, type **Axel Delgado** and click OK.

   Axel's effective permissions are displayed.

9. Take a screen capture of the Effective Permissions tab and save it as C:\Lab Manual\Lab 09\Labwork\Exercise9-6.bmp.

10. Click OK to close the Advanced Security Settings For Accounting Data dialog box.

11. Click OK to close the Accounting Data Properties dialog box.

12. Close Windows Explorer.

EXERCISE 9-7: DISABLING ANONYMOUS ACCESS ON THE DEFAULT WEB SITE

Estimated completion time: 15 minutes

Your manager has asked you to ensure that anyone who tries to access the company intranet site on \\server*xx* via Internet Explorer is prompted for a username and password before the Web site is displayed.

1. On the Administrative Tools menu, click Internet Information Services (IIS) Manager.

2. Expand the Server.*xx* node in the scope pane.

3. Expand the Web Sites folder.

4. Right-click Default Web Site and select Properties to display the properties for the default Web site.

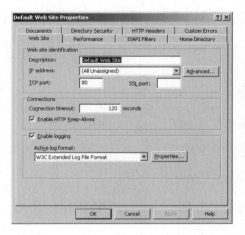

5. Select the Directory Security tab to open the security properties for the default Web site.

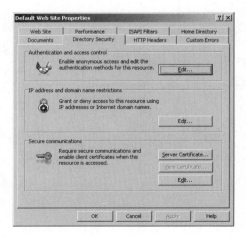

6. Click Edit in the Authentication And Access Control section.

The Authentication Methods dialog box opens.

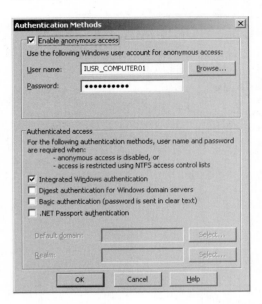

7. Clear the Enabled Anonymous Access check box.

8. Click OK to close the Authentication Methods dialog box.

9. Click OK to close the Default Web Site Properties dialog box.

The Inheritance Overrides dialog box appears.

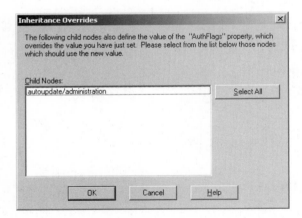

10. Click OK to close the Inheritance Overrides dialog box.

11. Close the Internet Information Services (IIS) Manager console.

12. Open Internet Explorer.

13. In the Address Box, type **http://Server*xx***.

You are prompted to log in before the Web site contents are displayed.

14. Enter the Administrator name and password.

   A Web site called Under Construction is displayed.

15. Close Internet Explorer.

16. Log off the computer.

EXERCISE 9-8: TAKING OWNERSHIP OF A FILE

Estimated completion time: 15 minutes

Maria Hammond has created a file in the Accounting Data directory and set the NTFS permission so that only she has full control of the file. She is on vacation for a week, and the accounting manager, Shane DeSeranno, needs access to the file.

1. Log on as Maria Hammond (mhammond).

2. Open My Computer from the Start menu, and browse to C:\Accounting Data.

3. Create a text file called Accounting Forecast.txt.

4. Open the Properties dialog box for the Accounts Forecast text file, and then select the Security tab.

5. Click Advanced to open the Advanced Security Settings dialog box.

6. On the Permissions tab, clear the Allow Inheritable Permissions check box.

   The Security dialog box opens.

7. Click Copy to copy the currently inherited permissions to the folder and close the Security dialog box, and click OK to close the Advanced Security Settings dialog box.

8. Select the Accounts Users group and click Remove.

9. Repeat step 8 to remove all groups and users besides Maria Hammond. This means that only Maria Hammond has Full Control.

10. Take a screen capture showing the permissions that you applied and save it as C:\Lab Manual\Lab 09\Labwork\Exercise9-8a.bmp.

11. Log off and log on as Administrator.

   QUESTION   Try to open the Accounting Forecast.txt file. Were you successful?

12. Open the Properties dialog box for the Accounting Forecast text file, and select the Security tab.

   A message tells you that you do not have permission to view or edit the permissions on this file.

13. Click OK.

14. Click Advanced to open the Advanced Security Settings dialog box.

15. Select the Owner tab.

16. Select Administrator, and click OK to take ownership of the file.

17. Click OK to close the Properties dialog box for the file.

18. Re-open the properties dialog box for the Accounting Forecast text file. It needs to be re-opened to show the changes made when you took ownership of the file.

19. Click on the Security tab to open the Security Properties and the Accounting Forecast text file.

20. Click Advanced to open the Advanced Security Settings dialog box.

21. Take a screen capture of the Owners tab and save it as C:\Lab Manual \Lab 09\Labwork\Exercise9-8b.bmp.

22. Click OK to close the Advanced Security Settings dialog box.

23. Set the permissions on the Accounting Forecast text file so that Shane DeSeranno can read and modify the contents of the file.

24. Take a screen capture of the Permissions tab and save it as C:\Lab Manual \Lab 09\Labwork\Exercise9-8c.bmp.

25. Close all open windows.

LAB REVIEW QUESTIONS

Estimated completion time: 5 minutes

1. If you have the share permission of Change and the NTFS permission of Read, what are your effective permissions?

2. You are a member of two groups, GroupA and GroupB. GroupA has the NTFS permission of Read & Execute to a file, and GroupB has the NTFS permissions Allow Write and Allow Modify. What are your effective permissions?

3. What are the five types of authentication methods available in Internet Information Server?

4. One of your users requires access to a share on the server on a daily basis. You have been asked to ensure that the user can access the share via a drive letter from My Computer. What steps would you take?

5. You have been asked to ensure that all members of your Marketing department have access to a share on your server. What would be the simplest method to assign the Marketing department permissions to the share?

LAB CHALLENGE 9-1: ADDING A FILE TO THE COMPANY INTRANET AND SETTING PERMISSIONS

Estimated completion time: 10 minutes

The Marketing department has created a new document called Demographics.htm and they would like it saved to the company intranet site. This file should be accessible by only the users in the Marketing department, and they should be able to access it through *http://serverxx/demographics.htm*.

1. Ensure that you are logged on as Administrator.

2. Copy the file demographics.htm from the C:\Lab Manual\Lab 09\Labwork directory into the C:\inetpub\wwwroot directory.

3. Set the permissions on the demographics.htm file (in the wwwroot folder) so that only members of the Marketing Personnel group have read access to the file.

4. Set the permissions on the demographics.htm file so that Maria Hammond has full control over the file, and ensure that Maria Hammond is the Owner of the file.

5. Take a screenshot of the permissions that you applied and save it as C:\Lab Manual\Lab 09\Labwork\Challenge9-1.bmp.

6. Open Internet Explorer and enter the URL *http://serverxx/demographics.htm*. When prompted for a username and password, enter the Administrator account and password.

   QUESTION   *Were you able to access the file?*

7. Close Internet Explorer.

8. Open Internet Explorer and enter the URL for the Demographics page; when prompted to logon, enter **mhammond** and the password associated with Maria's account.

9. The Marketing Demographics page should now be displayed.

   QUESTION   *What is the total number of leads?*

LAB 10
WORKING WITH PRINTERS

This lab contains the following exercises and activities:

- Exercise 10-1: Creating a Local Attached Printer
- Exercise 10-2: Configuring the Properties for a Local Printer
- Exercise 10-3: Sharing a Printer
- Exercise 10-4: Connecting to a Printer
- Exercise 10-5: Monitoring a Print Queue Using Performance Monitor
- Exercise 10-6: Clearing a Printer Queue
- Lab Review Questions
- Lab Challenge 10-1: Creating a Printer Pool

LAB DEPENDENCIES

To complete this lab, you must be sure that you have done the following:

- Completed all exercises in Lab 6 and Lab 7.

After completing this lab, you will be able to:

- Monitor print queues
- Troubleshoot print queues
- Create and share a local printer
- Connect a client to a network printer

Estimated completion time: 90 minutes

EXERCISE 10-1: CREATING A LOCALLY ATTACHED PRINTER

Estimated completion time: 10 minutes

You have been asked by your manager to install a new HP LaserJet 6P on the LPT1 port of your server.

1. Log on as Administrator.

2. On the Start menu, select Printers And Faxes.

    The Printers And Faxes window opens.

3. Double-click Add Printer.

    The Add Printer Wizard opens.

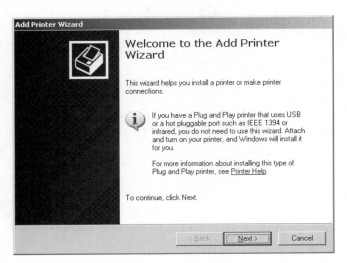

4. Click Next.

    The Local Or Network Printer page appears.

5. Select the Local Printer Attached To This Computer option.

6. Clear the Automatically Detect And Install My Plug And Play Printer check box.

7. Click Next.

    The Select A Printer Port page appears.

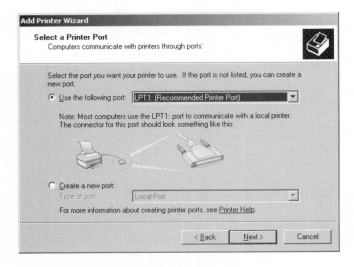

8. Leave the settings as the default, setting the printer to use LPT1, and click Next.

The Install Printer Software page opens.

9. Select HP from the Manufacturer column.

10. Select HP LaserJet 6P from the Printers column.

11. Click Next.

The Name Your Printer page opens.

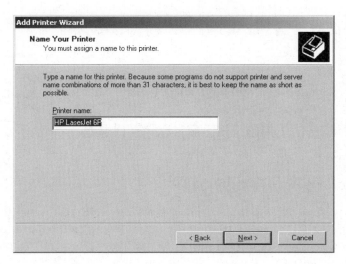

12. In the Printer Name text box, type **Accounts Printer** and click Next.

The Printer Sharing page opens.

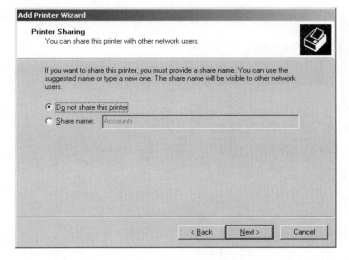

13. Select the Do Not Share This Printer option and click Next.

The Print Test Page page opens.

14. Select No, and click Next.

15. Take a screen capture of the Completing The Add Printer Wizard and save it as C:\Lab Manual\Lab 10\Labwork\Exercise10-1.bmp.

16. Click Finish.

Your machine copies the drivers needed for this new printer. Inform your instructor if you are prompted for any file locations.

17. An icon for your newly created printer appears in the Printers And Faxes window.

18. Right-click the Accounts Printer icon, and select Pause Printing.

EXERCISE 10-2: CONFIGURING THE PROPERTIES FOR A LOCAL PRINTER

Estimated completion time: 10 minutes

The new HP LaserJet 6P that you have installed is working well. You have just purchased some extra options for it: a 2 MB memory upgrade and two paper trays. You have been asked to configure the logical printer to use the extra memory and to use the first paper tray for DL Envelopes and the second tray for Legal Paper.

1. Right-click the Accounts Printer icon in the Printers And Faxes window, and select Properties.

The Accounts Printer Properties dialog box appears.

2. Select the Device Settings tab.

The Device Settings page for the Accounts Printer opens.

3. Click the underlined word *Letter* next to Tray 1.

4. Select Envelope DL from the Tray-1 drop-down list.

5. Click the underlined word *Letter* next to Tray 2.

6. Select Legal from the Tray-2 drop-down list.

7. Select 4 MB from the Printer Memory drop-down list.

8. Take a screen capture of the Device Settings page and save it as C:\Lab Manual\Lab 10\Labwork\Exercise10-2.bmp.

9. Click OK to close the Accounts Printer Properties dialog box.

EXERCISE 10-3: SHARING A PRINTER

Estimated completion time: 10 minutes

You have installed and configured the new HP LaserJet 6P. You have been asked to share this printer so members of the Accounts department can print to it.

1. Right-click the Accounting Printer icon in the Printers And Faxes window, and select Sharing.

The Accounts Printer Properties dialog box opens to the Sharing tab.

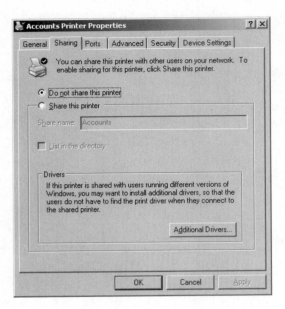

2. Select the Share This Printer option.

3. In the Share Name text box, type **Accounts**.

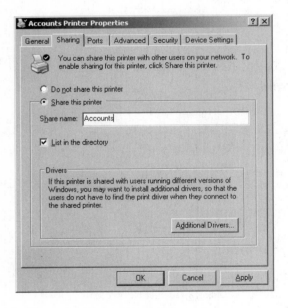

4. Select the Security tab, which shows the security settings for the Accounts printer.

5. Click the Everyone special identity, and then click Remove.

6. Click Add.

   The Select Users, Computers, Or Groups dialog box opens.

7. In the Enter The Object Names To Select text box, type **Accounts Users**, and then click OK.

8. Take a screen capture of the Security page showing the permissions for the Accounts Users group and save it as C:\Lab Manual\Lab 10\Labwork \Exercise10-3.bmp.

9. Click OK to close the Accounts Printer Properties dialog box.

10. Close the Printers And Faxes window.

11. Log off your machine.

EXERCISE 10-4: CONNECTING TO A PRINTER

Estimated completion time: 10 minutes

Maria Hammond wants to start using the new Accounts Printer, and has asked you to show her how to search Active Directory for printers and how to connect to a printer.

1. Log on as Maria Hammond.

2. Click Start, and select Search.

   The Search Results window opens.

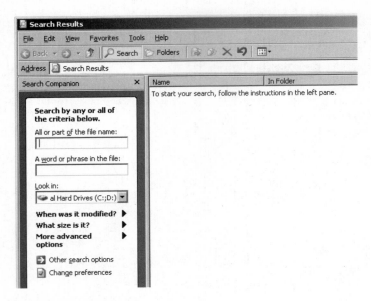

3. Click Other Search Options.

4. In the What Do You Want To Search For section, click Printers, Computers, Or People.

5. In the What Are You Looking For section, click A Printer On The Network.

   The Find Printers dialog box opens.

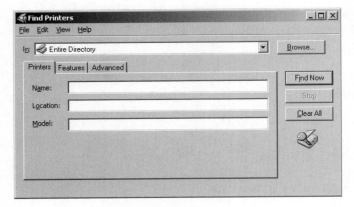

6. In the Name field, type **Accounts**, and then click Find Now.

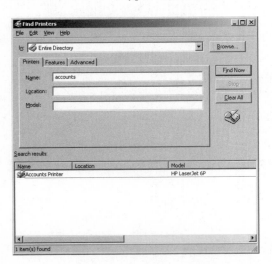

7. Right-click the Accounts Printer icon, and select Connect.

8. Close the Find Printers dialog box.

9. Close the Search Results window.

10. Click Start, and select Printers And Faxes.

   The Printers And Faxes window appears.

   QUESTION What indication do you get that the Accounts Printer is the default printer?

11. Close the Printers And Faxes window.

12. Open My Computer, and browse to the C:\Accounting Data directory.

13. Open the Maria Hammond.txt file in Notepad by double-clicking it.

14. Type your name in the text file, and save the file (CTRL+S).

15. On the File menu, select Print.

   The Print dialog box opens.

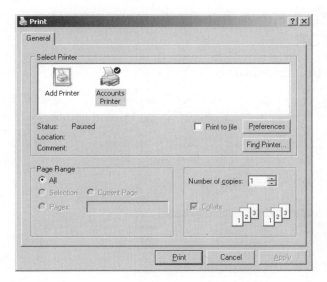

16. Click Print.

17. Close Notepad.

18. Close all open windows, and log off.

EXERCISE 10-5: MANAGING A PRINT QUEUE

Estimated completion time: 10 minutes

Maria Hammond has just printed a document by mistake, and she calls to ask you to stop it from printing.

1. Log on as Administrator.

2. Click Start, and select Printers And Faxes.

   The Printers And Faxes window appears.

3. Double-click the Accounts Printer icon.

The Accounts Printer manager is displayed.

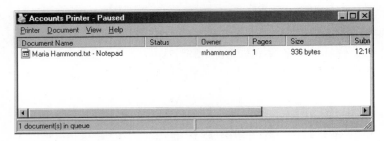

4. Right-click Maria Hammond.txt – Notepad, and select Pause.

QUESTION   What else can you do to Maria's document from the context menu?

5. Close the Account Printer window.

6. Close the Printers And Faxes window.

EXERCISE 10-6: MONITORING A PRINT QUEUE USING PERFORMANCE MONITOR

Estimated completion time: 20 minutes

You have been asked to provide management with some statistics about the Accounts Printer queue so they can determine if an additional printer is required.

1. On the Administrative Tools menu, select Performance.

The Performance console is displayed.

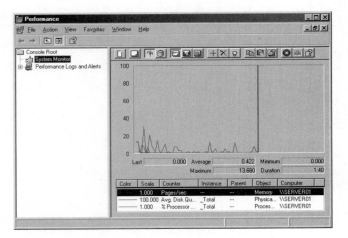

2. Select the Pages/sec counter object in the lower portion of the screen, and press DELETE. Repeat this for the remaining two counters. Your Performance console should look like this:

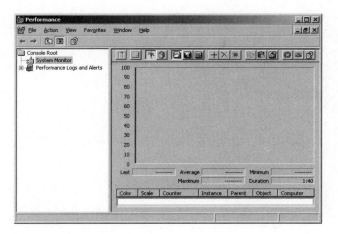

3. Right-click in the gray area in the details pane of the Performance console, and select Add Counters.

The Add Counters dialog box appears.

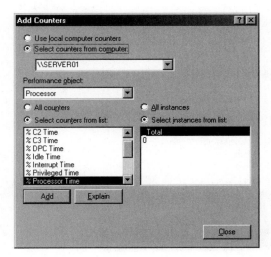

4. Select Print Queue from the Performance Object drop-down list.

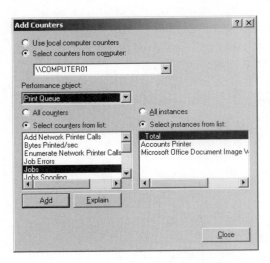

5. Select Jobs in the Select Counter From List drop-down list.

6. Click Accounts Printer in the Select Instance From List list box.

7. Click Add to add the performance counter to the Performance console.

8. Add the Jobs Spooling counter.

9. Add the Not Ready Errors counter.

10. Add the Out of Paper Errors counter.

11. Add the Total Jobs Printed counter.

12. Add the Total Pages Printed counter.

13. Click Close.

14. Minimize the Performance console. (Do not close it.)

15. On the Start menu, select Help And Support.

The Help And Support Center window appears.

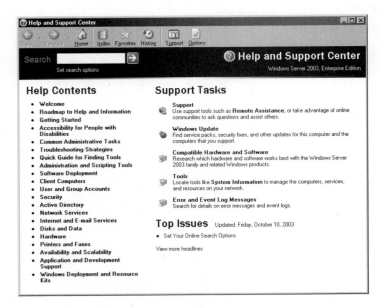

16. Click the Printers And Faxes link in the Help Content section.

17. Expand the Printing section.

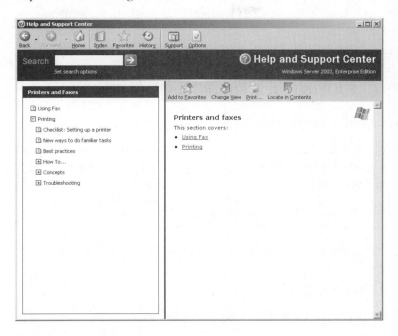

18. Click the Best Practices link.

The Best Practices text is displayed.

19. Click Print.

The Print dialog box appears.

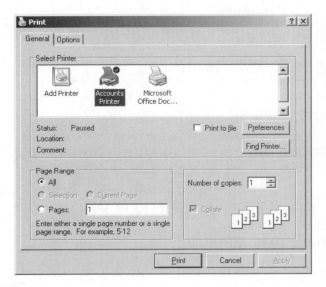

20. Click Print.

21. Click the Checklist: Setting Up A Printer link in Help And Support.

22. Click Print to open the Print dialog box, and then click Print again.

23. Close the Help And Support Center window.

24. Maximize the Performance window.

25. View your performance data in Report format by clicking on the graph and pressing CRTL+R.

26. Take a screen capture and save it as C:\Lab Manual\Lab 10\Labwork \Exercise10-6.bmp.

27. Close the Performance console.

EXERCISE 10-7: CLEARING A PRINTER QUEUE

Estimated completion time: 5 minutes

You have had problems with the Accounts Printer, and a number of documents have queued up. These documents were reprinted to another printer in your organization, so you have been asked to clear the Accounts Printer queue.

1. Open the Printers And Faxes window and double-click the Accounts Printer icon to open the Accounts Printer manager.

2. Select the first print job in the queue, hold down the SHIFT key, and select the last print job in the queue.

3. Right-click the selected jobs and select Cancel.

   A message box opens, asking if you want to cancel the selected print jobs.

4. Click Yes to confirm deletion of the print jobs.

5. Close the Accounts Printer manager.

LAB REVIEW QUESTIONS

Estimated completion time: 5 minutes

1. How do you configure the printer to use Tray 1 for envelopes?

2. The Accounting department in your company has five printers. Management has asked you to give them a report on the number of print jobs each printer produces so they can decide if all of the printers in use are necessary. How do you do this?

3. One of your users has three printers available to her (one color, one laser, one dot matrix). The user complains that she can only print to the dot matrix printer. How can you get her jobs to print to the laser printer?

LAB CHALLENGE 10-1: CREATING A PRINTER POOL

Estimated completion time: 10 minutes

You have just taken delivery of a new HP LaserJet 6P, and the Accounting department wants you to configure the logical printer for the Accounts Printer so that you have a printer pool comprising the original HP LaserJet 6P and the new one. The new printer will be connected to the LPT2 port.

After you're finished, take a screen capture showing the printer pool using both the old printer and the new one, and save it as C:\Lab Manual\Lab 10\Labwork \Challenge10-2.bmp.

LAB 11
MANAGING DEVICE DRIVERS

This lab contains the following exercises and activities:

- Exercise 11-1: Configuring Driver Signing Options
- Exercise 11-2: Installing an Unsigned Device Driver
- Exercise 11-3: Managing Device Properties
- Exercise 11-4: Using Last Known Good Configuration
- Lab Review Questions
- Lab Challenge 11-1: Using Device Driver Rollback

After completing this lab, you will be able to:

- Configure driver signing options
- Install and configure server hardware devices
- Monitor server hardware
- Configure device properties and settings
- Configure resource settings for a device

Estimated completion time: 60 minutes

EXERCISE 11-1: CONFIGURING DRIVER SIGNING OPTIONS

Estimated completion time: 5 minutes

Your manager has asked you to ensure that no unsigned device drivers are installed on your server.

1. Log on as Administrator.

2. Open Control Panel, and select System to open the System Properties dialog box.

3. Select the Hardware tab.

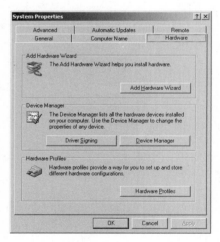

4. Click Driver Signing to open the Driver Signing Options dialog box.

5. Select the Block – Never Install Unsigned Driver Software option.

6. Click OK to close the Driver Signing Options dialog box.

7. Click OK to close the System Properties dialog box.

EXERCISE 11-2: INSTALLING AN UNSIGNED DEVICE DRIVER

Estimated completion time: 10 minutes

You have been asked to install an unsigned device driver on your server and to see what the effects will be on the system.

1. Select System from Control Panel to open the System Properties dialog box.

2. In the Hardware tab, click Device Manager.

The Device Manager window opens.

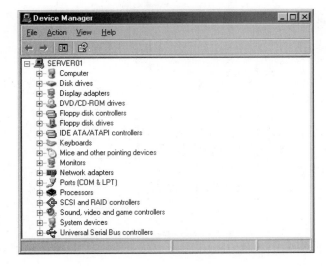

3. Double-click the Mice And Other Pointing Devices node to expand it.

4. Right click PS/2 Compatible Mouse, and select Update Driver.

The Hardware Update Wizard launches.

5. Select the Install From A List Or Specific Location (Advanced) option, and click Next.

The Please Choose Your Search And Installation Options page appears.

6. Select the Don't Search. I Will Choose The Driver To Install option, and click Next.

The Select The Device Driver You Wish To Install For This Hardware page appears.

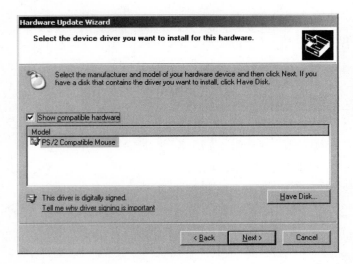

7. Click Have Disk.

The Install From Disk dialog box opens.

8. Click Browse.

The Locate File dialog box opens.

9. Navigate to C:\Lab Manual\Lab 11\Tools\MSMouse Driver, and select msmouse.inf from the list of files.

10. Click Open.

11. Click OK in the Install From Disk dialog box.

12. Click Next in the Hardware Update Wizard.

   A Confirm Driver Install dialog box opens.

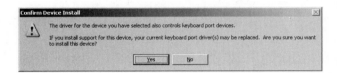

13. Click Yes.

   A Hardware Installation message box opens, indicating that the driver is unsigned and that the installation will not continue.

14. Take a screen capture of this message box, and save it as C:\Lab Manual \Lab 11\Labwork\Exercise11-2.bmp.

15. Click OK.

   The Cannot Install This Hardware dialog box opens.

16. Click Finish to close the Hardware Update Wizard.

17. Close the Device Manager window and the System Properties dialog box.

EXERCISE 11-3: MANAGING DEVICE PROPERTIES

Estimated completion time: 10 minutes

You recently installed a new piece of hardware in your server, and it conflicts with the LPT1 port on your machine. The manufacture of the new device suggests that you disable the LPT1 port.

1. Select Computer Management from the Administrative Tools menu.

   The Computer Management console opens.

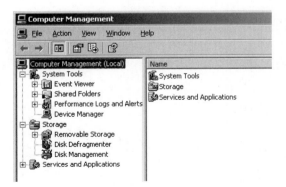

2. Select the Device Manager snap-in in the scope pane.

3. Double-click the Ports (COM & LPT) node in the details pane to expand it.

4. Right-click ECP Printer Port (LPT1), and select Disable.

   You will see a message box indicating that disabling this device will cause it to stop functioning.

5. Click Yes to confirm disabling the port.

6. The System Settings Change message box might open, prompting you to restart your machine. If it does, click No.

7. Take a screenshot of Device Manager in the Computer Management console, and save it as C:\Lab Manual\Lab 11\Labwork\Exercise11-3.bmp.

8. Close the Computer Management console.

EXERCISE 11-4: USING LAST KNOWN GOOD CONFIGURATION

Estimated completion time: 15 minutes

After making changes to your COM1 and LPT1 resources, you have noticed that your server has become unstable. Nobody has logged on to or off of the server since you made the changes. To bring the server back to its original configuration, you have been instructed to use the Last Known Good Configuration feature of Windows Server 2003.

1. Close all open windows.

2. Select Shutdown from the Start menu.

   The Shut Down Windows dialog box appears.

3. In the What Do You Want The Computer To Do drop-down list, select Restart.

4. In the Option drop-down list, select Hardware Installation (Planned).

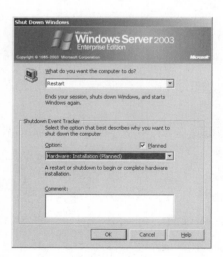

5. Click OK.

   Your machine restarts.

6. While your machine is rebooting, press the F8 key until the Windows Advanced Options menu appears.

   IMPORTANT   If you *do not see the* Windows Advanced Options menu but are instead prompted with the default logon screen, *do not log on*. Instead, cycle the power on your server and press F8 again, or seek the assistance of your instructor. If you log on, the setting made in the previous lab will become your Last Known Good Configuration.

7. Select Last Known Good Configuration (Your Most Recent Settings That Worked) from the menu, and press ENTER.

8. When prompted to select the operating system to start, select Windows Server 2003 and press ENTER.

   Your machine continues with the restart, and you are prompted to log on.

9. Log on as Administrator.

10. Select Computer Management from the Administrative Tools menu.

11. Select Device Manager in the scope pane.

12. Double-click the Ports (COM & LPT) node in the details pane to expand it.

   QUESTION   Is the LPT1 port still disabled? Explain why or why not.

13. Close the Computer Management window.

LAB REVIEW QUESTIONS

Estimated completion time: 5 minutes

1. Why did we set the driver signing options to Block?

2. You just added a new device driver to your system, and every time you try to log in, the system hangs. How can you fix this problem?

3. What two methods can you use to access Device Manager?

LAB CHALLENGE 11-1: USING DEVICE DRIVER ROLLBACK

Estimated completion time: 15 minutes

You have been asked to investigate the Device Driver Rollback feature of Windows Server 2003. You will need to set the Device Driver Signing options on your server to allow you to install an unsigned device driver.

1. Configure the Device Driver signing options for your machine to be set at Warn, and then update the Device Driver for your PS/2 Compatible Mouse using the Device Driver from C:\Lab Manual\Lab 11\Tools\MSMouse Driver. Then take a screenshot of the Drivers tab.

2. Roll back the Device Driver to the previously installed driver.

3. Take a screenshot of the Drivers tab once the rollback is complete.

4. Close all Windows, and log off your machine.

LAB 12
MANAGING DISK STORAGE

This lab contains the following exercises and activities:

■ Exercise 12-1: Creating a New Extended Partition

■ Exercise 12-2: Creating a New Logical Disk

■ Exercise 12-3: Converting a Disk from Basic to Dynamic

■ Exercise 12-4: Creating a Simple Volume

■ Exercise 12-5: Extending a Simple Volume

■ Lab Review Questions

■ Lab Challenge 12-1: Error-Checking and Defragmenting a Volume

LAB DEPENDENCIES

In order to complete this lab, you must be sure that the following is done:

■ You need at least 2 GB of unallocated space on your first hard drive.

After completing this lab, you will be able to:

■ Manage basic disks and dynamic disks

■ Optimize server disk performance

■ Defragment volumes and partitions

Estimated completion time: 65 minutes

EXERCISE 12-1: CREATING A NEW EXTENDED PARTITION

Estimated completion time: 10 minutes

You have been asked to create a new extended partition on your server using 1 GB of the available free space.

1. At the Run command, type **diskmgmt.msc**.

   The Disk Management console opens.

   NOTE   The Disk Management snap-in is included in the Computer Management console and can be added to a custom MMC. When it is added as a snap-in to a custom MMC, you can choose whether to use it to manage the local computer or a remote computer.

2. Right-click on the Unallocated section next to Disk 0 in the bottom pane of your Disk Management console, and select New Partition.

   The New Partition Wizard launches.

3. Click Next.

   The Select Partition Type page appears.

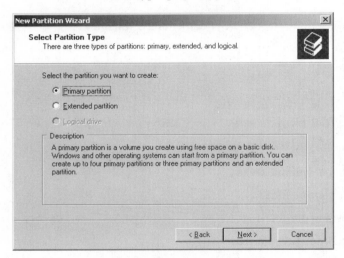

4. Select the Extended Partition option, and then click Next.

   The Specify Partition Size page appears.

5. In the Partition Size In MB control, type **1024**.

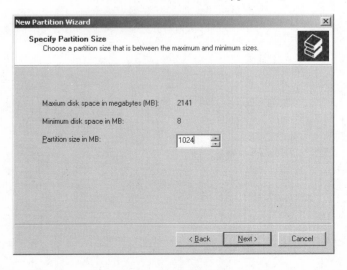

6. Click Next.

7. Take a screen capture of the Completing The New Partition Wizard summary page, and save it as C:\Lab Manual\Lab 12\Labwork\Exercise12-1.bmp.

8. Click Finish to close the wizard.

EXERCISE 12-2: CREATING A NEW LOGICAL DRIVE

Estimated completion time: 10 minutes

You have noticed free space on one of the drives in your server, and you have decided to make a new logical drive using some of this free space. The new logical drive will be 1 GB in size and formatted as FAT32.

1. In the Disk Management console, select the Free Space section of Disk 0. This is the free space on the extended partition that was created in Exercise 12-1.

2. Right-click on the Free Space section for Disk 0, and select New Logical Drive.

   The New Partition Wizard launches.

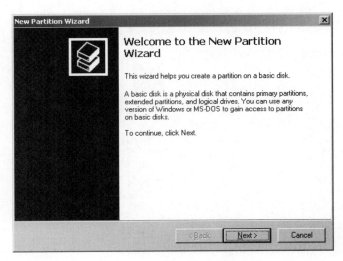

3. Click Next.

   The Select Partition Type page appears.

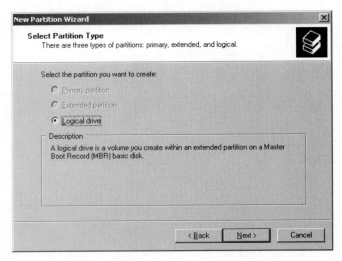

4. Ensure that the Logical Drive option is selected, and click Next.

   The Specify Partition Size page appears.

5. In the Partition Size In MB control, type **1024**.

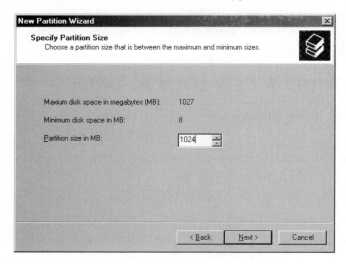

6. Click Next.

The Assign Drive Letter Or Path page appears.

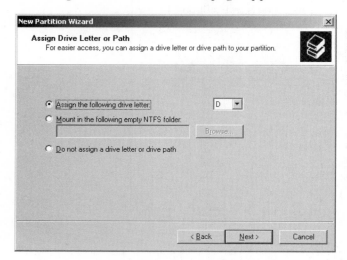

7. Leave the drive letter as the default, and click Next.

The Format Partition page appears.

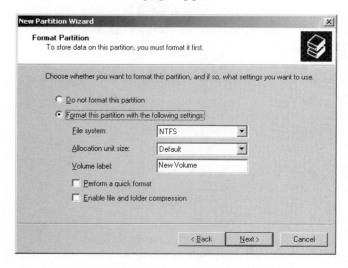

8. Leave the Format This Partition With The Following Settings option selected, and select FAT32 from the File System drop-down list.

9. In the Volume Label text box, type **DATA**.

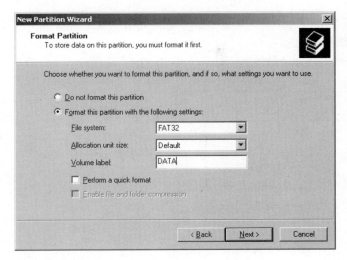

10. Click Next.

11. The Completing The New Partition Wizard summary page appears. Take a screen capture and save it as C:\Lab Manual\Lab 12\Labwork \Exercise12-2.bmp.

12. Click Finish.

The partition is created, and your system starts to format it. Do not perform any further tasks until the formatting is completed.

EXERCISE 12-3: CONVERTING A DISK FROM BASIC TO DYNAMIC

Estimated completion time: 10 minutes

Your manager has asked you to convert Disk 0 in your server to a dynamic disk so you can use the new features that dynamic disks offer.

1. In Disk Manager, right-click the Disk 0 icon in the lower part of your screen.

2. On the context menu, select Convert To Dynamic Disk.

The Convert To Dynamic Disk dialog box appears.

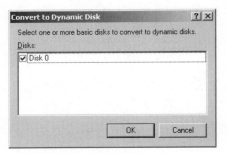

3. If you have multiple disks in your machine, ensure that only Disk 0 is selected.

4. Click OK.

   The Disks To Convert dialog box appears.

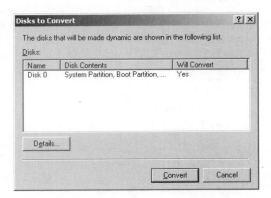

5. Click Convert.

   The Disk Management message box appears.

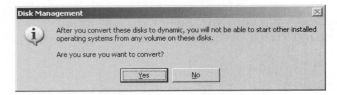

6. Click Yes to confirm the conversion.

   The Convert Disk To Dynamic message box appears.

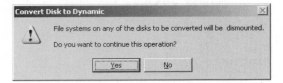

7. Click Yes.

   The Confirm message box appears.

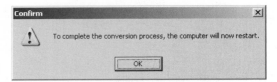

8. Click OK.

   Your machine reboots.

9. Log on as Administrator.

10. Open the Disk Management MMC.

   QUESTION   *Based on the information provided by Disk Management, what are the volume types of your two partitions?*

EXERCISE 12-4: CREATING A SIMPLE VOLUME

Estimated completion time: 10 minutes

Your manager has asked you to create an additional simple volume on your server called HOME. This volume will be used to store users' home directories and should be formatted as NTFS. Your manager has asked that the volume be 500 MB in size.

1. Open the Disk Management MMC, if it is not already open.

2. Right-click the unallocated disk space on Disk 0, and select New Volume.

   The New Volume Wizard launches.

3. Click Next.

4. In the Select Volume Type page, ensure that the Simple option is selected.

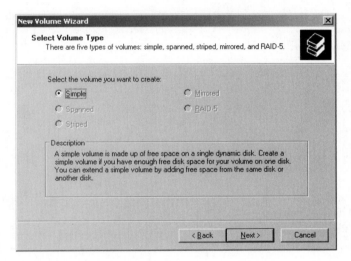

5. Click Next. In the Select Disks page, ensure that Disk 0 appears in the Selected list box. If it does not appear, select it in the Available list box and click Add. This list of disks includes only dynamic disks; basic disks do not appear in the list.

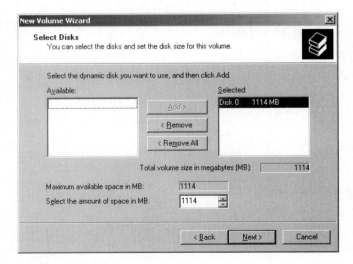

6. In the Select The Amount Of Space In MB control, type **500**, and then click Next.

7. In the Assign Drive Letter Or Path page, accept the defaults and click Next.

   The Format Volume dialog box appears.

8. Ensure that the Format This Volume With The Following Settings option is selected.

9. Ensure that NTFS is selected in the File System drop-down list.

10. In the Volume label text box, type **HOME**.

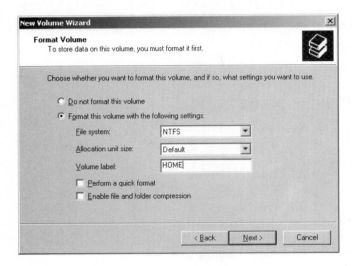

11. Click Next.

12. The Completing The New Volume Wizard summary page appears. Take a screen capture of the page and save it as C:\Lab Manual\Lab 12\Labwork \Exercise12-4.bmp.

13. Click Finish.

    Your new volume is created, and the system starts formatting the volume.

EXERCISE 12-5: EXTENDING A SIMPLE VOLUME

Estimated completion time: 10 minutes

After you've created the new volume called HOME, your manager asks you to make it larger. She wants the new volume to be 1 GB in size, not 500 MB as originally requested.

1. Right-click the simple volume called HOME, and select Extend Volume.

   The Extend Volume Wizard launches.

2. Click Next.

   The Select Disks page appears.

3. Ensure that Disk 0 is listed in the Selected column. (If you have more than one dynamic disk, you can select them from the Available list box and click Add; this enables you to extend the volume using space from multiple dynamic disks.)

4. In the Select The Amount Of Space In MB control, type **500**.

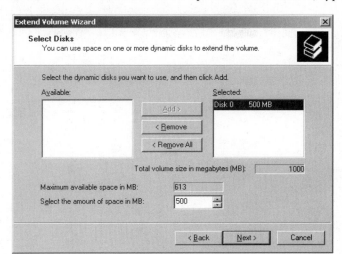

5. Click Next.

6. Click Finish to close the Completing The Extend Volume Wizard.

7. Take a screen capture of your Disk Management MMC and save it as C:\Lab Manual\Lab 12\Labwork\Exercise12-5.bmp.

LAB REVIEW QUESTIONS

Estimated completion time: 5 minutes

1. You have been asked to administer the disks on a remote server. What steps do you take?

2. You need to extend a simple volume. When you are prompted to select the drives to use, not all of your drives appear in the Available list box. What could be the reason for this?

3. You have been asked to convert one of your server's disks to dynamic. Why should you schedule this operation for nonworking hours?

LAB CHALLENGE 12-1: ERROR-CHECKING AND DEFRAGMENTING A VOLUME

Estimated completion time: 10 minutes

You have been asked to defragment the DATA volume on your server. Before you do so, you need to check the volume for errors.

1. Open the Disk Management MMC.

2. Perform the Error-Checking task on the volume called DATA.

   QUESTION   *What steps did you take to perform this task?*

   QUESTION   *What options are available to you when you perform an error check on the volume?*

3. Once the error-checking phase has completed, defragment the DATA volume.

4. Click View Report, and save the report as C:\Lab Manual\Lab 12\Labwork\Report.txt.

TROUBLESHOOTING LAB B
REVIEWING YOUR ENVIRONMENT

You are one of the network administrators for Contoso Pharmaceuticals. The company network consists of a single Active Directory domain named contoso*xx*.com (where *xx* is your assigned student number).

As the network administrator, you have the responsibility to ensure that resources (files, directories, printers, etc) are secured on Contoso's network. At present, all resources have been secured using individual user accounts, and this has become very ineffective since the network has experienced a large amount of growth. You have been asked to investigate the use of groups to secure resources. You have also been asked to ensure that all network resources have the required security settings to ensure unauthorized access is not possible.

Contoso is thinking of implementing a company-wide intranet, and you will be responsible for maintaining the security on it. The Intranet will be hosted on a Windows Server 2003 machine using Microsoft Internet Information Services.

The management for Contoso has just approved the purchase of some extra storage for your server, and you will be responsible for the implementation and management of the new storage.

Due to the rapid growth that Contoso has experienced, they have taken delivery of 50 new Windows XP workstations, and you have been asked to ensure that the workstations are successfully deployed to the users. In order to manage the workstations more effectively you have decided to create an organizational unit called Workstations, and all workstations on the network should be placed in this OU.

Security on the Contoso network has become a big concern for management, and they need you to ensure that when new hardware is installed, the device drivers used should be digitally signed. If the driver has not be digitally signed, it should be blocked from being installed.

1. Many of the workstations on your network are joined to the domain by using the Network Identification Wizard on the workstation and supplying the Administrator account's credentials to add the workstation to the domain. You have noticed that all the workstations that are added to the domain using this method are in the Computers OU in Active Directory Users And Computers. You need to ensure that all new workstations are placed in the Workstations OU by default. What would you need to do?

2. One of the technicians on your network recently installed a new network card in a user's Windows XP workstation. The network card driver was not digitally signed but the technician was still able to install it. What would you do to ensure that this cannot happen in the future?

3. A folder is created and shared as Marketing, and you added the Marketing group with all permissions except Full Control. Tai Yee is a member of the Marketing group, but you need to restrict his access so he only has the ability to read the contents of the Marketing directory. What steps would you take?

4. You have been asked to look into using Universal groups on Contoso's network to help with group management across domains. You have created two test domains in your lab; however, when you try to create a Universal group the option is greyed out. Why are you unable to create a Universal group in your test domains?

5. A new printer has been installed in the Accounts department. Its main purpose is to allow the payroll users to print to it at all times during the day. You would also like members of the Sales department to print to the printer but only between 6 P.M. and 8 A.M. What steps would you take to achieve this?

6. You have just updated the video driver on your server. The installation of the driver went OK and no errors were reported; however, when you boot the server the graphical interface starts to load and then hangs. You think it may have something to do with the video driver that you just installed. What can you do to get the server back to its original state?

7. Your new storage has just arrived and you are concerned that users will use more space on the storage system than they should. What can you do to ensure that space on the storage system is controlled?

LAB DEPENDENCIES

To complete this lab, you must be sure that you have the following:

- A machine that is running Windows Server 2003 and Active Directory. (Lab Exercises 1-1 and 1-2 cover the installation of Windows Server 2003.

- A user account for Maria Hammond, which has been added to the Account Operators group. This account was created in Lab Exercise 6-2 and added to the Account Operators group in Lab Exercise 6-3.

CHANGING THE COMPUTER CONFIGURATION

In this portion of the lab, you or your instructor will change the computer configuration to facilitate troubleshooting in the following section. Two break scenarios are presented in this section. Your instructor will decide which computers will be subject to which break scenarios.

TROUBLESHOOTING

In this portion of the lab, you must resolve a number of configuration issues created in the "Changing the Computer Configuration" section.

As you resolve the issues, fill out a Troubleshooting Lab Worksheet (found at C:\Lab Manual\TroubleshootingLabB\Worksheet.doc) and include the following information:

- Description of the issue.

- A list of all steps taken to attempt to diagnose the problem.

- What was the problem?

- What was the solution?

- A list of resources you used to solve the problem.

TROUBLESHOOTING BREAK SCENARIO 1

You have been contacted by a user who has reported that he is having problems logging on from one workstation on the network. The user has tried to log on from another workstation in the domain and is successful in logging on. The workstation that the user cannot log on from is Workstation03. You have been asked to investigate why the user cannot log on from Workstation03.

The company intranet has now been put in place, but none of the users on the Contoso network can access the intranet using http://Server*xx* as they have been instructed to. It is important that the company intranet be accessible to all users using Internet Explorer. Using your troubleshooting skills, investigate what the problem is and resolve it as soon as you can.

A new share called TECHSUPPORT has been created on the server. Maria Hammond has reported that she is unable to save documents in the share, which was designed so that members of the Administrators group and members of the Account Operators group could share information with each other.

TROUBLESHOOTING BREAK SCENARIO 2

One of the administrators on your network recently created a new directory called Research on the C drive of your server. Users are reporting that they are unable to see the share using My Network Places. When you log on to the server you can see the C:\Research directory in Windows Explorer, and the icon indicates that it is shared out. You must make this directory accessible to users on the network so they can access it via My Network Places or from the Run command as \\Server*xx*\Research.

The company intranet has been set up, but when users access it at http://Server*xx* in Internet Explorer, they are not prompted to provide any logon credentials.

Management has asked that you investigate this and ensure that users cannot access the company intranet without first authenticating.

To improve communication between the Account Operators and the Administrators, a directory called IT Reports was created and shared as ITREPORTS. Maria Hammond, a member of the Account Operators group, has called informing you that she is having problems with the share and asked if you could ensure that the appropriate access is given.